station

to

station

Other Books by Gary Jansen

The 15-Minute Prayer Solution

The Rosary: A Journey to the Beloved

Holy Ghosts

station to station

An Ignatian Journey through the Stations of the Cross

GARY JANSEN

LOYOLA PRESS.
A JESUIT MINISTRY

Chicago

LOYOLA PRESS.
A JESUIT MINISTRY

3441 N. Ashland Avenue
Chicago, Illinois 60657
(800) 621-1008
www.loyolapress.com

Scripture quotations contained herein are from the *New Revised Standard Version Bible: Catholic Edition*, copyright © 1993 and 1989 by the Division of Christian Education of the National Council of the Churches of Christ in the U.S.A. Used by permission. All rights reserved.

Cover art credit: Christ Carrying the Cross, 1538 (panel), Cranach, Lucas, the Elder (1472–1553) / Kunsthistorisches Museum, Vienna, Austria / Bridgeman Images

ISBN-13: 978-0-8294-4458-2
ISBN-10: 0-8294-4458-0
Library of Congress Control Number: 2016952705

Printed in the United States of America.
16 17 18 19 20 21 22 23 Versa 10 9 8 7 6 5 4 3 2 1

For Harry and Nana

Contents

Author's Note

Before we go any further, I want to be clear: this book offers a series of reflections and exercises on the *scriptural* Stations of the Cross. Unlike the traditional Stations you'll find exhibited in most churches, this version of the devotion focuses exclusively on events that are found in the Bible. Encounters such as Jesus meeting his mother or meeting Veronica, who wipes his face along his way to Calvary, while traditionally rich in imagery and feeling, do not actually appear in the Bible. The focus here is on Scripture because reading the word of God, the Bible, brings us even closer to the Word of God, Jesus.

In ancient times, rabbis would chew on little pieces of the Torah, believing that by taking the word of God into their bodies they would become more like God, holier. This sounds a lot like our Eucharist, when we take the Word of God, the bread and wine, into our bodies so that we can become more like Christ. All of this is to say that the scriptural Stations allow us to be in the presence of the sacred, in both word and in the Word, Jesus.

Foreword by Jennifer Fulwiler

I was sitting on a park bench in New York City when I realized that I was in the presence of a mystic.

Gary Jansen and I had agreed to meet for coffee, our first in-person meeting after years of e-mail correspondence. My trip to the city was short, and my schedule was overbooked, and I had arrived at the coffee shop a sweaty, disheveled mess after running through the streets of Manhattan. We grabbed our drinks and began walking to a nearby park, and as we moved through the crowds of the city, my mind was a jumbled blur.

I was stressed about my trip, about commitments at home, about work deadlines. I took it for granted that it's an unavoidable part of modern life to walk around feeling overwhelmed and frazzled. Certainly Gary must feel that way, I thought; he'd built an impressive career in the notoriously intense New York publishing industry and was currently working on a grueling schedule to hit a deadline.

Yet once we settled into the park bench, I noticed something about him, something rare that I don't often encounter in people living busy lives.

Peace.

What I saw in that moment, and have continued to see in the subsequent years of our friendship, is Gary's special awareness of spiritual realities. No matter how many distractions he has in his life—the pressures of an intense job, the long commute, the struggle to make time for family in the midst of it all—he somehow manages to remain conscious of God's presence. He is as relatable as the guy sitting next to you on the subway, yet he has the otherworldly insights of a cloistered monk.

And this is why Gary is the perfect person to walk us through the Stations of the Cross. It is too easy for us to view these pivotal moments in the life of Christ as distant stories, tidbits we relegate to the backs of our minds because they have no relevance to our daily lives. Do these moments that we vaguely remember from Sunday school have anything to do with us when we're taking our kids to a crowded playground or exasperated at a colleague who takes credit for our work? Gary shows us that the answer is yes—that an understanding of each station can transform even the most mundane moments into an opportunity to grow closer to God.

Introduction by
Jessica Mesman Griffith

One Friday afternoon when I was in graduate school in Pittsburgh, I wandered into a church where Catholic children were praying the Stations of the Cross.

I hadn't been to Mass in years. I was, innocently, just taking a walk on a beautiful, warm spring day after my first Pittsburgh winter. But when I opened the heavy doors of Sacred Heart, I suddenly and unexpectedly reentered my childhood, or at least the few years of life before my mother died and everything went wrong.

As a former Catholic schoolgirl, I was immediately overwhelmed by the smell of incense, the familiarity of the movements, the song, the repetition of the prayers. If I've ever been struck down to my knees in prayer in this life, it was at that moment, in that church, surrounded by schoolchildren clumsily intoning the "Stabat Mater." Every scar of suffering and grief flamed bright and new within me, demanded healing, attention, and yes, prayer. It was a feeling of enormous relief, and it was the moment I came back to the Catholic Church. I'm still here.

Kneeling in that pew, watching the kids, hearing their young voices recite the familiar prayers—"We adore you, O Christ, and we praise you. Because, by your holy cross, you have redeemed the world"—I remembered just how it felt to be the seventh-grader in the itchy kilt, huddled in a dim, shadowy church with my classmates on a sunny spring day. I remembered the silly cartoons of Christ on the pamphlets, the outline of his face on Veronica's veil. I remembered standing and kneeling in what seemed like endless succession and thinking, *How long can this go on?* Fridays in Lent in southern Louisiana meant warm weather and delicious fish dinners. I won't claim that I had anything holier or deeper than such physical pleasures (and discomforts) in mind.

I hadn't really known what we were doing there, but that day in Sacred Heart, it became suddenly clear. We were training for death.

That sounds awful, doesn't it? Too morbid? Too stereotypically Catholic? But yes, those days spent in the church, walking in the steps of the condemned and suffering Christ, prepared me, somehow, to walk with a dying mother when I was in eighth grade and to walk through a lifetime, after that, without her. I'd had no idea, as that girl in her itchy kilt, that my own passion was coming so soon.

Just as Gary Jansen reflects on Christ's Stations of the Cross upon seeing his young son's first skinned knee, we're all bound to die a thousand little deaths in our lifetimes, a thousand letting gos and saying good-byes, a thousand hurts and humiliations and abandonments that mark the paths we wind to our own final crosses. The details change, but every baby is born, as Christ was, for his Passion. The Way of the Cross is the spiritual practice that taught me the way forward and through that pain; it's a path I'm still treading.

The Stations of the Cross is a physical prayer—strength training, as Jansen notes—a growing of the muscles, figurative and literal. Our bodies come to know it like a dance: genuflect, stand, kneel. But it's also an intellectual prayer, a prayer of the imagination, and this is why we come to know it so deeply, perhaps even more deeply than we realize. Praying the Stations can give us access to strength, endurance, and hope when we find ourselves or ones we love in the midst of terrible pain.

The Stations teach us to suffer well. That doesn't mean our suffering will look good. There might be blood and sweat and tears and anguish. Or there might be hidden wounds that don't heal. Sometimes we'll limp (or be dragged) to the finish. But we can endure, forgive, pray, surrender—and even accept help on our way. Christ did all those things before us, showing us the way. Jansen reminds us that this way takes us to suffering that is not meaningless, to suffering that can be transformed and redeemed. This is the Way of the Cross.

In *Station to Station*, Jansen guides us through this rich, imaginative prayer. With each scriptural meditation, he invites us to enter a story that isn't yet over. He shows us how the events on Calvary are still unfolding in our lives, every day. We begin to see that "the spiritual life" is a redundant phrase; as Jansen puts it: "All of creation and all of our experiences are mysteriously infused with the Spirit of God. Everything is spiritual, from the person who is mysteriously cured of a disease to the mundane chores of the day, such as washing dishes."

When we enter fully, imaginatively, into these moments in the life of Christ—the critical moments that reveal the essence of his character, which is endless love and mercy—the process alters our imaginations, fine-tunes them to God. We begin to notice his fingerprints everywhere, echoes of the ongoing story all around us—in Bowie and Prince songs, too. Each of us is engaged in the unfolding of this epic, one that didn't end at the cross or the tomb or even the Resurrection.

Jansen reminds me that I have a part to play in this story, whether I like it or not. The choice to be made here is, how will I play it? Who will I be in the Passion today—helper, like Simon of Cyrene? Mourner, like the women weeping at the roadside? Judge, like Pilate, who'd really rather just wash his hands of the mess? Or is it my turn to suffer, to bear the cross, to die in small and large ways and be made new?

The Stations bring us right to that empty tomb, stone rolled away, revealing only darkness and shadows. We stand with Jansen and face the emptiness each of us has felt at some time or another, and we are reminded to trust even that emptiness. Because it's there, in what looks like nothing, that our greatest hope exists. God has moved there before, and he moves there still, every day.

No, it's not a morbid thing, this training for death. As Jansen walks with us from station to station, he points us from pain toward love and hope, toward strength and endurance, toward transformation. And we end up, all of us, resurrected.

PART 1

Why This Journey?

Man is created to praise, reverence, and serve God our
Lord, and by this means to save his soul.
The other things on the face of the earth are created for
man to help him in attaining the end for which
he is created.
Hence, man is to make use of them in as far as they help
him in the attainment of his end, and he must rid himself
of them in as far as they prove a hindrance to him.

—The Spiritual Exercises, 23

Imagine This . . .

You have my whole heart. You always did.
—Cormac McCarthy, *The Road*

Imagine for a moment the greatest love of your life. Your beloved. This person is the center of your existence, a person who makes you feel truly alive. Before you met your beloved, you were anxious, distracted, frail, broken. But now in your emerging love, you feel strong. You feel *alive*. You don't know what you were experiencing before, but it wasn't this. This person has helped you understand your past, and you are worrying less and less about the future. Instead, you are focused on the here and now. Everything you do, everything you experience, is saturated with *feeling*.

Continue to imagine your beloved. This person is a gifted teacher and not only has taught you how to live but also has touched the hearts of a community. The more lives this person influences, the more people flock to your beloved looking for inspiration. This is certainly a drain on the time your beloved spends with you, but for the first time in your life you don't feel jealous. You begin to realize that the more love is shared, the more love you have in your life. If you have an apple and cut it in half and give one piece of it to a stranger, you will have half an apple to eat. You may get hungry. But if you give half of your love away, you end up having twice as much love as you did in the first place. By giving, you gain.

Although your beloved has helped numerous people, there are others who have grown bitter, envious, and angry. They slander your beloved. They criticize; they mock and soon bring your love to trial. Certainly the storm clouds have been gathering for a while. You heard the rumblings of discontent. Your beloved acknowledged that these were dangerous times. But everything moves so fast. One moment you are having dinner with your love and your friends, and soon thereafter are betrayals, an arrest, an indictment, torture, and a sentence of death. All in less than twenty-four hours. Your mind keeps racing with the same question: *Why is this happening?*

Now imagine your world beginning to implode. Here is the love of your life, falsely accused and charged, being taken away from you. Your beloved has committed no crime. You are helpless. You feel useless. There is nothing you can do. The friends who have claimed loyalty to your beloved have turned their backs. You are not even allowed one final moment with your beloved. Instead, you will be forced to be a spectator to the execution. You feel completely alone.

Shadows deepen. Winds hiss. The sky turns the color of dirty bath water. The air smells of sulfur and ozone. A crowd begins to stir. You turn and in the distance see your beloved in the streets among a jeering, spiteful crowd—laughter crackles like flames. On your beloved's back is a beam of wood. You cry out in horror, but your voice is not heard. Empty birdsong.

The crowd is ravenous, held back by the arms of soldiers who have taken to the streets to keep the scene peaceful. Amid the chaos, a few people weep for your beloved, holding out their hands in support. You try to get closer to your love, moving among contorted faces, but the crowds are too deep. You catch a glimpse of your beloved struggling to walk. And then the falling. You want to help the love of your life, to ease the burden, to put an end to this madness.

But there is nothing you can do except watch and pray for mercy.

As hot tears run down your face and you feel your heart beating in your head, you hear a whisper in your ear: "It is only when the seed is broken that the tree begins to grow."

Stations of the Cross
as Spiritual Path

Who will connect me with love?
—David Bowie, "Station to Station"

The Stations of the Cross is a pathway to spiritual awakening. Too often we can journey through life asleep at the wheel, so to speak, oblivious to our own feelings or the lives of those who surround us on any given day. How often, for instance, have you commuted to work only to realize you don't remember how you made it to the front door of the fine establishment that employs you? As someone who has traveled to and from New York City via the Long Island Railroad for nearly twenty years, I know firsthand that unsettling feeling of lost time. More often than not, as the train proceeds along the Babylon branch, passing from station to station through the suburban and urban landscapes of Nassau and Queens, I am lost in thoughts I won't remember later in the day, worrying about a deadline, scrolling through my phone and watching the latest kitten video on Facebook, or just spacing out. Sometimes I read. Rarely do I pay attention to my fellow commuters, the countless people on the streets visible from the dirty train windows, leaving for or coming home from work just like me, or all the apartment buildings that house the lives of people I will never know but who laugh, cry, fart, and struggle through life just like everyone else.

Part of this myopia for me is certainly daily stress mixed with lack of sleep, tinged with a touch of perpetual acedia. Part of it is just plain old familiarity. (Two decades of traveling on the railroad can do that to you.) And while familiarity can, as the saying goes, breed contempt, it can also lead to a form of mental blindness and spiritual dementia. We think we're paying attention when we're not. We think we know something when really—let's be honest—we don't have a clue. We think we're normal when maybe—well, maybe—we're just a little crazy.

This happens quite often with matters of the soul, that indefinable part of us that looks to make sense of the sometimes beautiful and sometimes tumultuous world around us. This immaterial, invisible layer of metaphorical skin—what philosophers, theologians, and aging hippies call our essence—can at times feel stretched. We in turn feel weary, bored, and downright lazy. And while there are multiple ways to stimulate and engage this side of us, I've found the Stations of the Cross to be an antidote to those states of mind, a jolt out of complacency and a splash of cold water to the sleepy face of my soul. This meditation, a spiritual form of shock therapy, while not necessarily a new or upbeat practice—it does, of course, focus on the final hours of Jesus' first life on earth when he was mocked, beaten, and killed in a truly gruesome way—is nonetheless an invitation to the sacredness that lies in the beating heart of suffering, an appeal to inhabit a space of loss and to embrace loneliness, pain, fear, and betrayal: all friends we like to keep hidden in a locked basement or run away from if we can. It asks us not to look away from the train wrecks of life but to stop, consider, and stare eye-to-eye with the worst we can be—and also the best we are called to be.

The penultimate event in the Stations is Jesus' being raised on a cross for all to see. Crucifixion was meant to kill a person slowly, but it was also meant to be an embarrassment, a way of publically shaming an individual.

Yet two thousand years after the events that led to his death, Jesus is still held aloft in churches and in the outstretched hands of believers today. The cross not only is a reminder of what we can do to God through our own misdeeds but also is a symbol of courage, sacrifice, and the greatest act of love any of us can offer: to lay down our life for another. Jesus' suffering is ultimately a prelude to the symphony of the Resurrection. The cross isn't a sign of defeat but rather one of victory.

We Can Be Heroes

If, as the poet T. S. Eliot once famously wrote, time past and time present are perhaps contained in time future (meaning, essentially, that the boundaries of time are a lot looser than we might think), then the Stations offer another opportunity as well: to right a two-thousand-year-old wrong. Abandoned by almost everyone he held dear, Jesus spent most of his final hours without a friend or companion. By entering the Stations, we get the opportunity to journey back there, to be present with Jesus when no one else is, to be his compatriot as he makes his way to Calvary, to stand as a witness by his side, and to be a kind face that he looks upon when the loneliness of his ordeal is too much to bear. Prayers know no boundaries, and praying for and with Jesus on the cross, even though the events took place two millennia ago, still takes a bit of that pain away from him.

Many years ago, a noted psychologist asked a rather good-natured audience, "If I squeeze an orange, what comes out of it?" After a few seconds, someone shouted back,

"Orange juice!" The audience laughed. The psychologist smiled. "Yes," he said, "orange juice. Why?" A few moments followed, and another audience member answered, "Because that's what's inside the orange." There was a little more laughter, and the psychologist smiled again. "Yes, you don't squeeze an orange and get apple juice. You squeeze an orange and you get orange juice, because that's what's inside it. We could say the juice is the orange's essence." Audience members nodded and commented to one another about how true this was.

The psychologist then looked at the audience and asked another question: "So what comes out of you when someone puts the squeeze on you? When someone is mean or disappoints you or slanders you?"

Silence. No one answered. At least, not out loud.

Under Pressure

So, what comes out when someone puts the squeeze on us or treats us badly? What comes out of us when we're under stress? When things don't go as planned? When we're stuck in traffic? When we make a mistake at work? When our spouse, child, friend, or coworker disappoints us? When we're betrayed? When we could have sworn there was more money in the checking account, yet the check bounced? What comes out? Anger? Vitriol? Sadness? Depression?

Frustration? Fear? Revenge? I've experienced just about all those emotions, during disappointing and uncertain times. Goodness, what does that say about me? About what's inside of me? *Ick.*

For better or for worse, what comes out of us indicates our emotional, intellectual, and spiritual dispositions. It's kind of like this: Have you ever been on a highway and seen someone driving like a maniac? Tailgating? Speeding and weaving in and out of traffic? Would you say that person is healthy in the head or has problems? Maybe you say you can't answer that question, that you don't have enough information. But that car is an extension of the person's attitude. I'm not being judgmental. Maybe that person is having a really bad day—maybe he was laid off from work or lost his wallet and is trying to race back to the place where he may have dropped it. Still, that vehicle comes to express, through that person's actions, the attitude of "Hey, look at me! I'm acting like a fool." In the same way, how we respond to life and stress expresses who we are at any given moment.

So here's another question for you. What came out of Jesus when the world put the squeeze on him, when he was mocked, beaten, and crucified? There were tears. There was blood. There was water. But there were also strength, heroism, compassion, sorrow, resilience, gratitude, love, and forgiveness. There was nonviolence. There was peace.

Just as we can learn what is in an orange when it is squeezed, and just as we can learn more about who we are when we examine how we react to the challenges we face, we can learn more about Jesus by reflecting on what came out of him during the most intense period of his life.

The Stations, Past and Present

Composed of fourteen events that follow Jesus from the hours after the Last Supper until his crucifixion and entombment, the Stations of the Cross, also known as the Way of the Cross, is a mystical pilgrimage into the suffering heart of Christ and a unique pathway to spiritual awakening.

Popularized by the Franciscans in the thirteenth and fourteenth centuries, the custom of praying and meditating on the suffering of Christ probably dates back to the days following Christ's resurrection. Through the ages, followers of Jesus have passed down many stories while revisiting the sites in the Holy Land where Christ walked in the final moments of his life. One such story contends that Mary, the mother of Jesus, was seen walking and praying in the footsteps of her beloved son, tracing his final journey from the Roman praetorium, or Pilate's house, through the dry, cracked streets of Jerusalem to the "place of the skull," Golgotha, where the blood of Christ mixed with the desert sands. This path would in time come to be known as the Via Dolorosa, or the Way of Sorrows.

As this act of devotion grew in popularity, and as Christianity spread across the Mediterranean and Europe, more and more people were setting out on a pilgrimage to the Holy Land to walk in the footsteps of Christ. But during the Middle Ages and times of the Crusades, Jerusalem became a dangerous place as Christian and Muslim armies warred in the name of God. During this time, many of the clergy began erecting symbolic stations in local churches so that the faithful could make spiritual pilgrimages while staying close to home. The Stations of the Cross became, then, a series of paintings, illustrations, or sculptures that depicted the final scenes of Christ's earthly life. Though there were many variations on these events throughout different communities—some were based on passages in the New Testament, while others were popular stories that had been handed down from generation to generation—the stations that most of the faithful have been reciting for hundreds of years are what we call the traditional Stations.

The Traditional Stations of the Cross

Jesus is condemned to death.

Jesus is made to carry the cross.

Jesus falls the first time.

Jesus meets his mother.

Simon helps Jesus carry the cross.

Veronica wipes Jesus' face.

Jesus falls the second time.

Jesus speaks to the mourning women of
       Jerusalem.

Jesus falls the third time.

Jesus is stripped of his garments.

Jesus is nailed to the cross.

Jesus dies on the cross.

The body of Jesus is taken down from the cross.

The body of Jesus is laid in the tomb.

In 1991, Pope John Paul II, wanting to give believers an alternative set of stations upon which to pray and meditate, proposed a new list based solely on events described in the New Testament.

The Scriptural Stations of the Cross

Jesus prays in the Garden of Gethsemane.

Jesus, betrayed by Judas, is arrested.

Jesus is condemned by the Sanhedrin.

Jesus is denied by Peter.
Jesus is judged by Pilate.
Jesus is scourged and crowned with thorns.
Jesus bears the cross.
Jesus is helped by Simon of Cyrene to carry
          the cross.
Jesus meets the women of Jerusalem.
Jesus is crucified.
Jesus promises his kingdom to the good thief.
Jesus speaks to his mother and the disciple.
Jesus dies on the cross.
Jesus is placed in the tomb.

Though traditionally considered a meditation on suffering, the Stations of the Cross is more than a simple, ancient act of piety. It is a portrait of grace under pressure, a collection of specific reactions from Jesus during times of crisis. In our current age of global terrorism, economic uncertainty, widespread and severe depression and anxiety, and environmental devastation, the Stations offer us an opportunity to strengthen our souls and grow the mystical muscles of our hearts. Using the basics of Ignatian prayer, in particular imaginative prayer, we can hop aboard a time machine that takes us back to the final moments in Christ's life. Here, we can not only meditate on sorrow but also ask two essential questions: how did Jesus respond to suffering, and how do we?

Suffering is a reality for all of us. Instead of asking why it happens (the answers, no matter how eloquent and thoughtful, are always unsatisfying), let's change the questions and explore how we can respond to anxiety, pain, and disappointment as Jesus would, and then apply some of those principles to our own situations. The answers you receive will radically change your life. I know. It happened to me, but more on that later.

Sounds like a plan, right? But, if you're like me, you might think that Jesus has an unfair advantage over us. As Christians, we believe Jesus was fully human, but he was also fully God! That had to take the edge off the nails and thorns just a little, right? Of course he could withstand the torture—he's *God,* for goodness sake! Me? I cry if a little hot olive oil splashes on my arm while I'm cooking breakfast.

Yet our faith reminds us that Jesus (*sans* all the miracles) was like us in many ways: he craved food and water as we do, cried as we do, and got tired and needed to rest. He was tempted as we are, and he even lost his patience from time to time. Though he was God incarnate, he was more like you and me than we might suspect.

My goal is not to reduce the Stations to a checklist of noble and heroic goals we must strive for. This path is not a pursuit of perfectionism. Just as Jesus stumbled and fell during this life, so do we stumble and fall. We are imperfect. We make mistakes. Yet the more we spend time with Jesus as he endures the hardships of the Passion, the more we realize that a journey back in time to the cross helps us relieve the burden of the cross for our fellow travelers on the spiritual path—simply by helping our own souls. Most of the time we're not in a prayerful, meditative, or contemplative state. We're dealing with bills, jobs, headaches, and annoying people at the grocery store. Yet the Stations give us an opportunity to step out of our ordinary lives. It can be so easy to sleepwalk through life, to pass by and not pay attention to the suffering around us. The Stations speak to us by saying, "Hey, slow down, walk with me, I have something important to show you." Focus on his suffering and reactions, and you will definitely be changed.

As Pope Francis often reminds us, Jesus meets us where we *are*. And in our encounters with Christ, with all our shortcomings and limitations, we have the opportunity to grow stronger and more courageous, which in turn helps us become more aware of and merciful to others. Just imagine Jesus as the sun. If we hide in the shadows, the world looks like a very dark place. But if we move to a clearing and let the sun shine on our faces, we feel its warmth and we can see things in all their heavenly glory.

How the Stations
Changed My Life

The point of intersection of the timeless
With time, is an occupation for the saint.
—T. S. Eliot, *Four Quartets*

I experienced a fair share of abuse while growing up, which left me with an odd form of self-diagnosed post-traumatic stress disorder. There are times when I'll be walking down the street only to flinch or dodge an imaginary blow that just isn't there; call it bad memories, call it phantom pain, call it whatever, but it's real and unsettling. I stayed clear of the Stations for a big part of my life. Though I knew there were people out there who suffered worse than I did, I still wanted nothing to do with meditations or prayers that had to do with misery. Give me the Joyful and Glorious Mysteries of the rosary—those were more my speed. Keep the sorrowful stuff to yourself, Lord.

But some years ago, I found myself alone with my grandmother in her hospital room. I was watching her die. Though

I kept a strong face, I was sad, frightened, and confused. For much of my life, my Nana (sometimes "Nana Banana," a nickname I gave her when I was a small child) was a second mother for me—a lighthouse in the tempest—always there with a smile, some words of encouragement, or a small bag of my favorite pretzels (my snack of choice after school for many years). Though she lived simply, she struggled her whole life, always on the verge of poverty, always dealing with uncertainty. When her husband, Harry, my grandfather, a grave-digger for more than thirty years, died of a heart attack when I was twenty-two, it became my time to take care of her in some ways. I was just starting out in my career and busy with work and making new friends at my new job, but I would take Nana to the grocery store every week, primarily to get cat food (I swear her cats ate more food than she ever did) and to Calverton National Cemetery once a month to visit Harry. At the time, I was driving an old Jeep CJ-7, and in the summer we'd take off the hard-shell roof and cruise down the Long Island Expressway en route to the old flower shop she loved so much; there we would buy the perfect bouquet of cash-and-carry carnations to put on my grandfather's grave.

Nana. We were pals. We were, in many ways, best friends.

The last five years of her life, though, had become even more of a struggle than the first seventy-eight years. She suffered a series of strokes and became bedridden. Her daughter, my aunt, who had struggled her whole life with addiction, became her primary caregiver. During those final years, because of various complicated circumstances, I didn't see my grandmother very much. We would talk on the phone from time to time, but visits were almost impossible. I missed those old days when we were BFFs, blasting Bruce Springsteen on the radio while she wore big bug-eyed sunglasses, giving people the peace sign as we cruised to the grocery store.

But here she was now, so close to death. She couldn't speak. Her hospital room was quiet except for the beep of the heart monitor and her own labored breathing. I knew I was going to lose her, and I knew I was going to lose her soon. I took her frail, soft hand into mine and just held it as I looked into her eyes. For a fleeting moment I felt her whole life flash in front of me. *Wait*, I thought afterward, *isn't that supposed to happen when I die?* But at the moment I felt as if all her stories—growing up in Brooklyn, her walks on the boardwalk at Coney Island, all the Pepsis she bought for a nickel, the death of her father when she was twenty-one, the loss of her first love, working at Woolworth's during World War II, the disappointments she suffered, the joys she experienced—had all been downloaded through the palm of my hand and into my heart. No words were spoken, but just being in her presence while she was suffering made me feel closer to her than I had ever felt before.

Nana would die a few days later. I wasn't in her hospital room when it happened, but to this day, I carry her life around inside me and I am a better person for it. Having been there with her during those painful moments created a bond and an understanding that continues to affect my life.

Sometime later, after her funeral, I was drawn to the Stations of the Cross. I don't know why. I just remember being in church and looking at the stained-glass depictions of Jesus' last moments. I thought of my grandmother and her struggles, and I looked at the colorful images as sun streamed in, casting an aquarium of colors on the floor, and I realized that just as I had felt close to my grandmother as she made her way to God, I felt closer to Jesus as I spent time with him as he inched his way to God. I'd never felt that before. It was late summer, and I remember asking myself why the Stations were relegated to Lent, when suffering is around us all the time. Soon thereafter, I made the Stations a regular exercise.

I love the visual representations of Jesus' life. As a movie geek and someone who attended film school for a couple of years, I like to look at the Stations of the Cross as if I were watching a movie while listening to the director's commentary. As Christians, we celebrate Jesus' Passion every year, so we may fall into the trap of thinking that we know the story, like, "Hey, I've seen this movie before; I know what happens."

But there's so much more going on that we might not know. When we meditate on the Stations, we give God the opportunity to speak about what's unfolding before our eyes: "Okay, in this scene, we see Jesus in the garden. He's in bad shape. He knows he's going to die soon, so he starts crying and praying to God. What Jesus doesn't see is that his friends have fallen asleep just outside the garden. He'll find out. But right now, he has no idea. Still, and you can't see this because the focus is really on Jesus, there is a whole group of angels watching over him. He thinks he's alone. He's not alone. He's never alone and neither are you." When we use imaginative prayer in our Stations meditation, we are given new insights into an old story. More on this soon.

The Stations Move Us from Old Life to New Life

The Stations of the Cross is ultimately a journey of self-emptying. As we walk with Jesus toward Calvary, we see that he keeps leaving more and more of his old life behind. Only days before his crucifixion, he had been welcomed in Jerusalem as a celebrity—a hotshot miracle worker who was inspiring thousands and challenging the establishment. Shortly thereafter, he lost most of his friends, his popularity, his clothes, his dignity, and his life. Yet all of this allowed Jesus, supported by beams of wood, to rely solely on God the Father.

Is this how Jesus wanted things to end? We can say that, because he was God, this is absolutely the way he wanted it. But if we're being honest, then the best we can say is that we just don't know. We have to remember that, at the start of the Stations, Jesus acts a lot like you and me. He prays to God to spare him from being put to the test. He doesn't want to suffer. But he knows that his life is not about him. "Yet not my will," Jesus says, "but your will, Father."

We, too, leave things behind as we make our way along the path we're given in this life. It's been said that there will be a time when the world stops giving us things and starts taking them away. We know that as we get older we may leave behind loved ones, old friends, homes, jobs, our health, our hair, our enthusiasm, and our memories. Yet as in Jesus' life, all these losses bring us closer not to self-reliance, as Henry David Thoreau might have it, but to God-reliance. The deeper awareness that comes from meditating on the Stations sets us free from having the world just the way we want it. Our expectations, or rather our attachments to our expectations, become barriers to joy. Allow me to share a silly but powerful example from my own life.

Not too long ago, my wife and I took our two sons to a local and very popular playground. We thought we'd get there early enough, before the place became overrun with other people's children. But no such luck. As we pulled into the parking lot, it seemed that at least fifty other families had the same idea: get to the park early before other people's raga-muffins arrive.

We got out of the car and walked to the gate of the park. What a disappointment. We had been talking about this trip all week and were looking forward to having full access to everything, but already there were long waits for the swings and the slides, and there wasn't much room to run around at all. Disappointed, I looked at my family and said, "Let's get out of here."

As we turned back toward the parking lot, one of my sons said, "I want to stay. Let's just play anyway. I'm Batman and you're the Joker and all these kids and their parents are patients at Arkham Asylum. Tag—you're it!" And off he ran. My other son followed, and so did my wife, and within seconds I was chasing the three of them through the crowds. Soon I was no longer in a crowded playground but in the crowded streets of Gotham looking for my archnemesis.

God was saying to me, "Drop your expectations and just have fun with your kids."

And I did.

The Stations and Social Justice

Making the Stations of the Cross a regular practice throughout the year is important because it is not only a spiritual exercise—and like any exercise it has the potential to strengthen and reshape us—but also an active meditation on social justice that helps to increase our awareness and concern for God's creation.

The cross of the first century that held Jesus aloft was made of wood and nails, but today that cross is forged of cold industrial steel, and it bears the weight of millions, if not billions, of people. On the cross today are the rejects, the losers, the fallen away, the destitute, the depressed, the lonely, the assaulted, the beheaded, the junkies, the freaks, the geeks, the bullied, the impoverished, the sick, the lost children, the minorities, the queer, the odd, the transgendered, and all the men and women who shuffle over the potholed bridges of life. All the people who are crucified by society, by terrorists, by big business, by you and me in the mindless things we sometimes do, are on that cross too. Flip off another driver on the highway. You just nailed that person to the cross. Mumble vitriol against someone under your breath. Nailed another. Pass someone on the street in need of help. Nailed. Ignore your kids. Nailed. There's an old saying that it's lonely at the top—well, not if it's the top of the cross.

Though Jesus seems passive throughout his Passion—he never lifts a finger against anyone and he barely speaks—his acceptance, forgiveness, and nonviolence are nonetheless revolutionary, providing first-century countercultural insight on how to live justly in the twenty-first-century world. We can see this in how he reacts in each station:

> Jesus in the Garden of Gethsemane. **He prays.**
> Jesus, betrayed by Judas, is arrested. **He is calm.**
> Jesus is condemned by the Sanhedrin. **He is steadfast.**
> Jesus is denied by Peter. **He accepts others' weaknesses.**
> Jesus is judged by Pilate. **He is quiet.**
> Jesus is scourged and crowned with thorns. **He is broken.**
> Jesus bears the cross. **He endures.**
> Jesus is helped by Simon of Cyrene to carry the cross. **He allows others to help.**

Jesus meets the women of Jerusalem. **He thinks of others.**

Jesus is crucified. **He feels pain.**

Jesus promises his kingdom to the good thief. **He forgives.**

Jesus speaks to his mother and the disciple. **He watches over his family.**

Jesus dies on the cross. **He weeps.**

Jesus is placed in the tomb. **He loves.**

To live out social justice, we have to feel what others feel, accept our own situations with grace and hope, face up to the evil around us, reach out to those who need us, and answer evil with love. Jesus' responses through the journey of the Stations show us how to respond to trouble, pain, and others' sins and needs.

What Makes This Journey Ignatian?

St. Ignatius asks us to seek God in all things. But in the Stations of the Cross, God seems to be missing. As Jesus makes his journey through the way of sorrows, he is at his most human. There are no miracles here. No sudden healings. No casting out of demons. No parables. Someone coming to the story of Jesus' Passion for the first time, not knowing anything else of the Gospels, would think that this is just an ordinary person, someone who experienced loneliness, heartache, pain, exhaustion, and ultimately death. He's no different from any of us. There's nothing extraordinary here, someone might think, except the amount of abuse leveled against this man and his determination to die with dignity.

What does this tell us? Many things, but what strikes me most is that the Passion asks us to find Jesus in the midst of loneliness, heartache, pain, and exhaustion as they occur in our own lives. We are called to seek God in *all* these very human things, these broken places and vacant rooms where we think God is not present. In modern times, with terrorism, racial strife, and police shootings seemingly all around us, how are we to find God in the midst of all this chaos, anger, and sadness? The answer is a most difficult one. Yet the Stations of the Cross can provide an answer that is at once practical and mystical. Journeying in the presence of Jesus at his most human does something to us spiritually: it helps us see Jesus' character, offering suggestions through his example of how to respond to suffering. And it also mysteriously alters our spiritual DNA, lifting us up, not on a cross, but into the arms of Jesus. In that embrace we are transformed in ways that make us better people.

The journey in the pages that follow is offered as a way of activating that practical and mystical experience by helping us to be, as Ignatius asked, attentive to God in all ways. Not tomorrow or yesterday, but now in this very moment. In the thoughts, stories, and questions for reflection that follow, I hope to do what Ignatius asks all of us to do: engage the mind and the heart and discern the presence of God in the here and now. The connection between the two creates a current of awareness that helps move our focus away from our own wants and desires to the wants and desires of God: that we stay awake, listen, serve, and love our neighbors in their suffering and in spite of our own.

In the chapters that follow, we will take an Ignatian approach that involves prayer, meditation, the imagination, our physical senses, and the practice of reflection. By applying these gifts to our journey, we will experience it more fully. We will walk alongside Jesus and, in doing so, meet God where we most need divine presence and help.

Imagination as a Key to Prayer

Ignatius knew a thing or two about the imagination. One of the most effective and eye-opening journeys through the Stations is the path of imaginary prayer, the process of composing a scene in your mind and engaging in it as if it were real. You can do it any time and any place. This way of praying is at the heart of Ignatian spirituality, which ultimately seeks God in all things, whether in nature, at church, in books, or in the highly imaginative thoughts of a young child.

Imagine is a truly powerful word. If I ask you to read a book, I am asking you to engage your intellect. If I ask you to look at a picture of a bird, you use your faculty of sight. If I ask you to listen to an old David Bowie song, you use your hearing. But if I ask you to imagine a cook preparing your favorite meal, in an instant all of your senses are engaged. You might hear the chopping of celery or the sizzling of butter in a pan. You might smell the aroma of onions. You might feel the heat of the oven and salivate because the scene you are imagining becomes so strong that your body has an involuntary reaction to it. What happens in the end is that a series of imagined sensory events becomes a unique and creative physical experience.

Ignatius realized that the imagination could transform the events of Jesus' life into personal and emotional experience. As David Fleming puts it in *What Is Ignatian Spirituality?*, "To follow Jesus we must know him, and we get to know him through our imagination. Imaginative Ignatian prayer teaches us things about Jesus that we would not learn through scripture study or theological reflection. . . . It brings Jesus into our hearts." Let's do a quick experiment. Read these lines:

> Now the chief priests and the elders persuaded the crowds to ask for Barabbas and to have Jesus killed. The governor again said to them, "Which of the two do you want me to release for you?" And they said, "Barabbas." Pilate said to them, "Then what should I do with Jesus who is called the Messiah?" All of them said, "Let him be crucified!" (Matthew 27:20–23)

Now imagine that scene. What does the crowd look like? How many people are in the crowd—thirty or three hundred? What do all these people sound like? Describe the expressions on their faces, the colors of their clothing. What time of day is it? How does Jesus react when he looks out at the people around him? Is he sad? Disappointed? Unmoved? Brave? Is there a smile on his face? Just stay with the images you've created for a few moments. Then ask yourself how you would feel if that were you on display. Stay with that response a moment and then let it go.

How do you feel? I know when I've done this exercise, I feel overwhelmed. It's a warm day, the sun is out, bleaching the surrounding buildings. The crowd is frenzied. In my imagination, Jesus is a bit horrified. As he looks out to see how everyone has turned against him, his heart feels like it's going to collapse. His throat goes dry. As I imagine this scene, I feel Jesus' fear. On more than one occasion, doing this exercise with the Stations has brought me to tears.

Now, you might be saying, "This is all fantasy. It's all made up! How does this bring me closer to God? And if I feel something, how do I know it's God and not just me making this up?" Well, even the best-selling author James Martin has had similar reservations about imagined prayers, questioning how fantasy could be a path to God. Even though it was a technique highly praised by Ignatius and has worked for countless people over the course of almost five hundred years, Martin, a Jesuit, still had reservations. In time, though, he began to realize that when Ignatius said to seek God everywhere, he meant it. Martin discerned that if God can speak to us through our intellect and through others' insights, certainly, then, he can talk to us through our imaginations. "Using my imagination," he writes, "wasn't so much making things up as it was trusting that my imagination could help lead me to the one who created it: God. That didn't mean that everything I imagined during prayer was coming from God. But it did mean that from time to time God could use my imagination as a way of communicating with me."

Moreover, just because something is imagined doesn't mean it is unimportant. C. S. Lewis's *The Screwtape Letters* is an imagined book, but it gives us some of the greatest insight into sin ever written. *The Lord of the Rings* is pure fantasy but demonstrates great truths about good, evil, heroism, and honor. Sylvester Stallone's character Rocky has inspired millions to never give up, whether in sports, at work, or when dealing with illness. Even Disney's popular movie *Frozen*, based on a classic fairy tale, has inspired countless children and young people to be strong and compassionate in their daily lives. Just because something is imagined doesn't mean it's not real and powerful.

In the pages that follow, each station is presented with a reading from Scripture as well as some brief reflections on what the scene tells us about Jesus' character. In addition, *Station to Station* offers ideas on how to use imaginative prayer to engage Jesus' pilgrimage as an exercise in simply awakening a new awareness of a story that many of us think we already know. Yet what is presented are simply suggestions. On your own, you might want to imagine yourself as Jesus in these exercises. Or maybe Pilate. Or a nameless bystander. Or perhaps you imagine a friend embodying Jesus, someone you've seen abused or falsely accused by others. Maybe you imagine the homeless beggar you see every day or one of your favorite celebrities who is being slandered by tabloid media. Maybe you see a soldier being led away by terrorists to his execution. Maybe you find yourself weeping alongside the women of Jerusalem. While this book offers some ideas, it's your decision how you move through the story.

Prepare for the Journey

Don't die without knowing the cross.
—Prince, "The Cross"

Anyone who has tried to pray or meditate knows it can be quite difficult. It seems simple: get quiet. Speak to God. Listen. Repeat. Yet anyone who has ever tried to silence his or her mind has probably struggled to do so. There seems to be so much chatter inside our heads. We try to stop thinking, but we just can't. This doesn't happen only during prayer. How many times have you been at a movie, a concert, or listening to a friend and, even though you want to pay attention to what's going on in front of you, your mind starts to wander . . .

Squirrel! Wait, what was I saying?

It's so easy to get distracted. I wish there was an easy way to turn down our internal volume.

Here's a technique you could try before we start our prayer. I've found it helpful to do a simple *reverse* breathing exercise. Yes, reverse. Most breathing techniques begin with,

"Take a deep breath in and let a deep breath out." That can certainly calm our minds, but switching the order of the breathing actually forces you to do something a bit out of the ordinary, which automatically shifts your focus away from the incessant chatter going on in your head. Give it a shot. Breathe out through your mouth, then in through your nostrils. That's one beat. Try it for eight beats.

This may feel odd, and that's the point. Although you're still breathing normally, your focus is on an unfamiliar pattern. Your head focuses so much on the strange breathing rhythm that your inner voice is quieted.

Most of the time we can't get rid of all the things racing around in our minds—that's totally normal. Just try to notice when your focus slips off the meditation, and gently bring yourself back to the scene before you. The Stations provide a time for you to spend with Jesus in conversation and presence, so try to focus as much as you can. You don't want Jesus thinking about other things if he's spending time with you, right?

When you are ready to begin your journey, start by making the sign of the cross (more on this later), and read the Scripture passage. As you do, begin tracing the steps of the Passion, allowing yourself to enter each scene through your imagination. Maybe you are a bystander, Christ's friend, his mother. You can imagine that you yourself are Christ:

- What do you see?
- What sounds do you hear?
- What emotions do you experience?
- What do you smell?
- What taste is in your mouth?
- How does Christ's Passion affect you today? Does it? Should it?
- What is *your* cross to bear?
- Ask the Holy Spirit for help to lift the weight.

Now, let's turn our attention for a minute to what I think is one of the most overlooked devotions of all time: the sign of the cross. While the action of moving your hand from your head to your chest to each shoulder is often taken for granted at the start of our prayers, the sign is a road map to a deeper spiritual life. Here's what I mean.

Our journey through the Stations begins with a reading from Scripture, which is essentially a mental exercise. The sign of the cross begins with intoning "the Father" and touching the forehead. We begin our imaginative prayer by reading words of Scripture with our *minds*, allowing the words to penetrate us intellectually. We should *think* about the

Scripture passage. What's going on? What does it mean? How does this relate to other stories I've read in the past? Then, following the path of the sign of the cross, we allow those words and thoughts to move to the Son, to the heart. Embrace a particular station in Jesus' life by *feeling* it, by engaging the emotions and the senses. We do this, as mentioned before, through Ignatian techniques of imaginative prayer. For example, when we encounter the women of Jerusalem halfway through the Stations, we can imagine what these women are feeling as they weep for this battered man on his way to execution. We can imagine Jesus' face as he looks at the people around him with a mixture of anguish and determination. Maybe we imagine angels supporting his body. We can imagine the shouting of the crowd, the cold looks of the soldiers. Pictures can create emotions, and by visually expanding each scene in our minds, we can access feelings that can ultimately bring us closer to God.

But the journey doesn't stop there. We must allow the Holy Spirit to pierce our hearts, symbolized in the movement of our hand from our left shoulder to our right shoulder. As you say, "and the Holy Spirit," imagine an arrow of grace from an unseen bow penetrating your heart. The mind and the heart can do only so much. We must then surrender to the experience of grace in order to stop focusing on our thoughts and feelings and just be. Let the experience settle in you. When we do this, it leads to the greatest affirmation of all time, the amen, the holy yes, "so be it," that comes at the end of our prayer.

Keep the stages of the sign of the cross in the back of your mind as you journey from station to station.

Last, the Stations of the Cross serve as an allegory for the journey through the spiritual life. By this I simply mean that hard times are often followed by good times. There are moments when we feel alone and exposed, but even though the Stations end with Jesus being laid in a tomb, the story doesn't end.

And beyond saying that the Stations help us along the way in our journey through "the spiritual life," we could simply say "life." All of creation and all of our experiences in life are mysteriously infused with the spirit of God. Everything is spiritual, from the experience of being mysteriously cured of a disease to the mundane chores of the day, such as washing dishes.

Many times, we want instant answers when we pray, but after years of praying on a regular basis and much time spent in spiritual exercises, I've discovered that God rarely gives us answers during these moments of quiet exchange. It's almost as if God needs to digest what we have to say and get back to us later. God needs to think about it. So instead of looking for instant answers, just be present to God, listen, speak if necessary, and then be silent. You might hear something, but more often than not, the answers come in the hours and days after prayer time. The best advice is this: pray the Stations, meditate on them, then go about your day—and pay attention. In your hours of work and study and searching, God is working supernaturally to bring you closer to the heart of Jesus. Indicators of these tiny miracles might be found in a song or a coworker's advice or a TV commercial, in a bird's call or a friend's kind words, or even in traffic. Just trust that God will guide you along the way.

God will.

PART 2

Now We Go, with Jesus

Think of his meek silence. This will be your effort. He will do the rest. He will do everything that's missing. But you have to do that: hide your life in God with Christ. This is done with the contemplation of the humanity of Jesus, of suffering humanity. There is no other way; there is none. It is the only one. To be good Christians, contemplate the humanity of Jesus and suffering humanity. To give testimony, in order to be able to give this testimony, that's what we need. To forgive, contemplate Jesus suffering. In order not to hate your neighbor, contemplate Jesus suffering, in order not to gossip against your neighbor, contemplate Jesus suffering. The only way. Hide your life with Christ in God: this is the advice that the apostle gives us. It is the advice to become humble, meek, and good, magnanimous, tender.

—Pope Francis

The First Station: Jesus Prays in the Garden of Gethsemane

Then Jesus went with them to a place called Gethsemane; and he said to his disciples, "Sit here while I go over there and pray." He took with him Peter and the two sons of Zebedee, and began to be grieved and agitated. Then he said to them, "I am deeply grieved, even to death; remain here, and stay awake with me." And going a little farther, he threw himself on the ground and prayed, "My Father, if it is possible, let this cup pass from me; yet not what I want but what you want."
—Matthew 26:36–39

Jesus' Response: He Prays

Imagine for a moment that you knew you were going to die tomorrow. Not only are you going to die, but also you're going to suffer. No falling asleep and quietly slipping away during the night. You are going to be mocked. You are going to be beaten. You are going to be tortured. You are going to be mutilated. You are going to be exposed to the elements. And then you are going to be asphyxiated slowly, in front of your mother.

While this may seem like the final scene from a Quentin Tarantino movie, we know this to be the story of Jesus' Passion. It's a story that's been told so often that many of us have become desensitized to its brutality and the sheer, vile evil that human beings inflicted on the Son of God. This is terrifying on many levels but none as much as this: if society can do this to God—*God!*—what's preventing society from doing it to me or you?

We have no idea when, exactly, Jesus knew he was going to suffer this death, but we do know that the Last Supper sets in motion the events that would lead to his crucifixion and then the miracle of his resurrection. For Jesus, in that moment, the events that are to unfold must weigh heavily on his mind as he breaks bread and shares wine with his friends. But how does he respond? Does he mock his enemies? Does he get angry and overturn the table or tackle Judas to the floor? No, he takes a few friends and he goes off to pray. Feeling grief and agitation, he asks his companions to hold vigil while he turns to his father.

Jesus is returning to the scene of the crime—the garden, the place where Adam and Eve committed the first sin. Gardens are supposed to be beautiful, quiet places, but here, in Gethsemane, the garden is a place of pain. We can imagine Jesus' sobs, and we can imagine him crying and shaking. He's afraid. He doesn't want to be alone: "I am deeply grieved, even to death; remain here, and stay awake with me."

I don't know about you, but if I had some idea that I was going to suffer the way Jesus did, I'd try to escape. Most of us would probably do the same. Even Jesus asks for a way out, to "let this cup pass" from him. Jesus may be the Son of God, but he doesn't want to suffer. Nonetheless, he ends his prayer with the simple affirmation found in the heart of the prayer that Jesus taught us to pray: "not what I want but what you want." In other words, "Thy will be done."

Most of my life, I'd been riddled with anxiety. These words of the Our Father, "thy will be done," made me tremble. "Thy will" could mean anything I *didn't* want. So, even though I had gone to Catholic school for twelve years, I was a bit of a slacker when it came to prayer, for no other reason than that it just didn't resonate with me. But in college I started spending more time reading the Bible and such mystics as St. John of the Cross and St. Ignatius of Loyola. In time, through good friends and good books, I started to pray more regularly—at first, though, only during times of stress. It would be a few years before I would move toward praying to God during good times as well. As I learned to lower my defenses, to put my trust in God more and more, I realized that by not praying I was preventing Jesus from being a part of my life and giving me strength when I needed it most.

I'd like to say that after I started to communicate with God on a regular basis, all my problems went away, but, well, they didn't. Yet, God and prayer put those problems in perspective. When we make God our center, our problems are put into perspective. This is not to say that they go away. Like a backseat driver, they can pressure you to "make this turn, make that turn, go faster, slow down." So annoying. But if we pray and put our focus on God, do those voices in the back really matter? Our destination is up ahead, and we're going where God is leading us, even if it means taking a turn we didn't expect.

We don't know if Jesus expected everything that unfolded in his life, but we do know that here in the garden he experiences his fears. He suffers. But as he turns his face to God, he focuses attention on the Creator, and by doing so, he's given strength. He is given peace.

Not what I want, God, but what you want.

Encountering Jesus

Imagine that you are Christ in the garden. Imagine how you would pray to God. Jesus would use the word *abba*, or "daddy," when he spoke to his father. This term of endearment shows an intimacy that Jesus had with God. If you were Jesus, what would you pray for? How would you react if you knew you were going to suffer? How does God respond? What feelings bubble up inside you?

Now, focus on a problem you have in the present. It could be a health concern or a tense atmosphere at work. It could be an ongoing argument you're having with a friend or spouse. Instead of focusing on the problem, instead of putting your attention on the pain, surrender those feelings and turn to God; let your first reaction be a prayer. How do you do this? Simply relax your shoulders (you probably didn't realize they were in a state of tension), take a deep breath, and intone the name of Jesus. When you are ready, speak to God from your heart.

We see in this station and in numerous other places in the Gospels that Jesus prays often. Make this commitment to yourself: pray every day. Don't have time? Well, set an alarm on your cell phone for 3:00 p.m. from Sunday to Monday. When the alarm goes off, take a few moments and talk to God, pray a part of the Chaplet of the Divine Mercy, say an Our Father, or just take a few moments to be still and know that God is present.

Take These Words to Prayer

"Father, if thou art willing, remove this cup from me; nevertheless not my will, but thine, be done." And when he rose from prayer, he came to the disciples and found them sleeping for sorrow, and he said to them, "Why do you sleep?"

—Luke 22:42–46

Review This Experience

Later today, or even tomorrow, spend a few quiet moments remembering what it was like to meditate on this station. Which emotions were dominant? What aspect of the experience stands out for you now?

Imagine
"In Gethsemane"

The coldest night of the year. A transparent moon hangs in the sky. Beneath it, a garden like the one where your ancestors played. You cry into your hands. There are whispers in the dark and the spirit of another watching over you. You remember a young child, walking in the cool breeze by the sea with his mother and father. There were twelve rocks in the boy's pocket, small ordinary stones taken from the shore, from the streets. You remember the child crying when he lost one. The twelfth is missing, the boy said. Now there are only eleven. His father beside him, touching his hair. His mother holding him in his arms, a prescient embrace. Her neck like the smell of roses.

The deep air, a waking dream. The cup before you.

Is this yours? a voice asks, trying to lift it. *So heavy for such a small thing.*

Don't touch it. Put it down. You don't want this. This is not how things were supposed to be. There was a promise of something else.

Your stomach burns. A strange sweat on your lips. *Please*, you say. *I cannot bear it.* Then, a quiet voice. The wind, the perfume of flowers, touches your hair. *You can. You must.* You see a stone moving, giving way to light.

Your will, you cry. *I will.*

The Second Station: Jesus, Betrayed by Judas, Is Arrested

While he was still speaking, Judas, one of the twelve, arrived; with him was a large crowd with swords and clubs, from the chief priests and the elders of the people. Now the betrayer had given them a sign, saying, "The one I will kiss is the man; arrest him." At once he came up to Jesus and said, "Greetings, Rabbi!" and kissed him. Jesus said to him, "Friend, do what you are here to do." Then they came and laid hands on Jesus and arrested him.
—Matthew 26:47–50

Jesus' Response: He Is Calm

If you're like most people, you have been betrayed. Maybe a friend or family member lied to you. Maybe someone you trusted started a rumor. Maybe you confided a secret to someone only to have that person share it with others.

I used to think that such experiences created emptiness inside us. But now I think that what really happens is that we gorge on inner talk that bloats us and essentially prevents us from moving in proper directions. We all know how sluggish we become if we eat too much. Well, betrayal not only scars us but also leads to our feasting on negative emotions. And in this state, we often want to lash out. We become angry, hostile, maybe even vengeful.

Some years ago, a former colleague of mine took credit for a project into which I had put a lot of time and effort. I was angry and wanted to lash out, and for weeks I carried this burden with me. Now, by *burden* I don't mean the betrayal. Part of me wasn't surprised at what happened. The person was sort of a Lex Luthor figure in my life. He could sometimes be my friend and biggest champion and then, a moment later, turn on a dime and undermine all I had done. No, the burden was that I wanted this person to suffer, and I was coming up with really lame ideas about what to do.

(I guess revenge isn't really my thing—my ideas to rearrange his office furniture or order a pizza to be delivered to him at 3:00 a.m. just made a coworker snicker.) Still, I was a bundle of nerves, and as much as I wanted to get on with my life, I felt stuck.

But what do we see in the Gospels and in this particular station? Jesus encounters Judas and calls him "friend." We don't know if Jesus is being sincere or intentionally ironic, but he doesn't slander his betrayer. He doesn't try to pummel him to the ground. Instead, he reacts with calm equanimity: "Do what you are here to do." We encounter Jesus in stillness. Having prayed in the garden only moments before, Jesus knows that whatever is going to happen next, God has his back. Even if his friends abandon him, God is with him at all times.

How would your life be different if you could live with that level of confidence, exude that much calm? One of my favorite stories from the Gospels is when Jesus says that if you have the faith of a mustard seed, you can move mountains. A mustard seed is one of the smallest seeds in the world. But how many of us are moving mountains? Peter had that seed for a moment when he walked on water. But, all too human, he dropped it along the way and fell into the sea.

Yet those seeds of faith are on offer to us all the time, and we can access them not by being full of wild emotions but by being still. I don't mean that you can't move around or go about your day-to-day duties but instead that you can experience peace in times of difficulty, knowing that God is with you.

Do not worry. Consider the lilies.

Encountering Jesus

Imagine for a moment that you are Jesus. It is night. You feel a slight wind on your face and neck. In the distance, you see a crowd of people with torches coming your way. Soon you see that your friend Judas is leading the group, and you know that someone you've walked with, listened to, eaten with, and shared your life with has sold you out to your enemies. We see in the Gospel story that Jesus is calm, but how about you? How are you feeling? Has this happened to you before? What were those experiences like? How did that burden weigh you down? How did you react?

Imagine that you are Judas walking toward Jesus. This is a man you've called a friend. What are you thinking as you lead these people to the man you know won't even resist arrest? Look into Jesus' eyes and ask yourself, *When have I betrayed another? Why am I doing this?* Pray for forgiveness.

Take These Words to Prayer

Jesus teaches us in his Sermon on the Mount not to be anxious. Reflect on the following passage. Memorize it. Pray to God to place these words in your heart.

Look at the birds of the air; they neither sow nor reap nor gather into barns, and yet your heavenly Father feeds them. Are you not of more value than they? And can any of you by worrying add a single hour to your span of life? And why do you worry about clothing? Consider the lilies of the field, how they grow; they neither toil nor spin; yet I tell you, even Solomon in all his glory was not clothed like one of these. But if God so clothes the grass of the field, which is alive today and tomorrow is thrown into the oven, will he not much more clothe you—you of little faith? Therefore do not worry, saying, "What will we eat?" or "What will we drink?" or "What will we wear?" For it is the Gentiles who strive for all these things; and indeed your heavenly Father knows that you need all these things. But strive first for the kingdom of God and his righteousness, and all these things will be given to you as well.

—Matthew 6:26–33

Review This Experience

Later today, or even tomorrow, spend a few quiet moments remembering what it was like to meditate on this station. Which emotions were dominant? What aspect of the experience stands out for you now?

Imagine
"Betrayed by Judas"

Middle of the night. Moonlight pours through a web of cypress trees. They have barely sprouted this year.

Flares in the distance, torches like stars in outstretched hands. I have been wondering when you would arrive. Old friend. Weak chin, sallow face, bony arms. You look older than I remember. At supper you were a boy with a secret, silver eyed and restless. Now, you stare at me like a scarecrow after harvest.

Something has always trailed you. I felt it earlier tonight. I feel it now. Even as you move closer, I feel its presence feather your heart. You have always been a beam of splinters. You have punctured the skin of all who drew near you. I have known about this for some time. When there was talk of mercy, I would watch your tiny looks, almost imperceptible. The subtle grimace, a narrowing of the eyes, a quiet laugh in the back of your throat.

You always kept your distance. But tonight you are the only brother to touch me. You are the last. And with a kiss. Dry. Punctured. The first nail.

They take me.

The Third Station: Jesus Is Condemned by the Sanhedrin

Now the chief priests and the whole council were looking for false testimony against Jesus so that they might put him to death, but they found none, though many false witnesses came forward. At last two came forward and said, "This fellow said, 'I am able to destroy the temple of God and to build it in three days.'" The high priest stood up and said, "Have you no answer? What is it that they testify against you?" But Jesus was silent. Then the high priest said to him, "I put you under oath before the living God, tell us if you are the Messiah, the Son of God." Jesus said to him, "You have said so. But I tell you, from now on you will see the Son of Man seated at the right hand of Power and coming on the clouds of heaven." Then the high priest tore his clothes and said, "He has blasphemed! Why do we still need witnesses? You have now heard his blasphemy. What is your verdict?" They answered, "He deserves death."
—Matthew 26:59–66

Jesus' Response: He Is Steadfast

When I was growing up, we had a number of velvet Jesus pictures in our house. The one I remember the most hung in my parents' bedroom for years. It was a picture of Jesus standing in profile, looking out over a city. Maybe this was painted to depict one of his temptations in the desert, when Satan tries to convince Jesus to become ruler of the world, or maybe it depicted him at a quiet time in contemplation. As I got older, I would look at that picture from time to time and wonder what was going on in his mind. Was he thinking about God, his father? Was he thinking about his friends? What really stood out for me was just how centered Jesus seemed to be. It was as if he were part of that mountain—unwavering, resolute, and strong.

We see these character traits of Jesus clearly in this station. Jesus is presented before a rather intimidating governing body of individuals—in my mind, I imagine Jesus like a young Jimmy Stewart, standing before Congress in *Mr. Smith Goes to Washington*. He's standing in the midst of hypocrites, those who say they uphold the law but are really self-preservationists. Moreover, there are supposed holy men present, and they are breaking the commandment about bearing false witness against your neighbor. It's a den of thieves.

Challenged by the chief priests, does Jesus back down? No. He stands with conviction, remaining silent for most of the interrogation and then turning the Sanhedrin's questions back on them.

You may think there is an air of superiority in Jesus' actions. And maybe you're right. But it's not flawed superiority, the feeling that you are better than someone else or know more than others. That's vanity, plain and simple. Jesus *is* superior here because he's permanently aligned with God.

When we are put into a difficult situation, how often do we feel the need either to back down or to defend ourselves? Personally speaking, I never want anyone to think I'm an idiot or to look at me critically. I'm, admittedly, a people pleaser. (Be kind—it's something I'm trying to change!)

I work in New York City, and while it's not quite right to call it a secular city (there are plenty of people of faith here, though sometimes they can be hard to find), it is a place that can feel quite Godless. Among my secular and atheist friends, I sometimes feel the need to defend my beliefs, to explain to them why I think the way I do and why I worship the way I do. What a waste of time! My heart, in these instances, is misaligned. I'm not trying to help them understand "spirituality," and goodness knows I'm not trying to convert them. I just feel insecure being the outsider, and I'm trying to protect myself. It's all fear wrapped in a shiny veneer of vanity.

But in this station we see Jesus' fearlessness. He's defiant in the face of hypocrisy. When he speaks, he does so succinctly and eloquently. He knows that God is always with him. He puts first things first—not the opinions of others but his relationship with his father.

Many self-help books tell us to believe in ourselves. We're told that if we believe in ourselves, then there's nothing we can't do. The sentiment is well intentioned but misguided. Instead, we should believe in God, follow the commandments, be merciful, and then there's nothing we cannot do. This doesn't mean that we're better than anyone else; we don't need to be arrogant about it. Feelings of superiority lead to, as they say in *Star Wars*, the dark side. But when we align ourselves with God in humility and stand firm, we never have to be afraid of who we are.

Encountering Jesus

Imagine Jesus standing before a tribunal. What is his posture? Look into his eyes. What are they revealing to you? Imagine that you are Jesus and that you're looking out at this sea of faces who hate and despise you. What is your reaction to them?

Imagine you're one of the crowd, and before you stands Jesus. You know this man has done nothing wrong, but look around you and see the faces of the people who want to condemn him. What do they look like? How does the room feel? What are people doing? You know that your words about this Jesus could further inflame those around you, leading to his death. What do you do? What are you thinking? Then imagine that the person in front of you isn't Jesus. Instead, it's a misfit, an outsider. Pick a person you know who you believe has been wrongly accused of being slow, lazy, stupid, dirty. What do you say to this person? How does it feel to interact with him or her?

Take These Words to Prayer

Therefore, my beloved brethren, be steadfast, immovable, always abounding in the work of the Lord, knowing that in the Lord your labor is not in vain.

—St. Paul, 1 Corinthians 15:58

Review This Experience

Later today, or even tomorrow, spend a few quiet moments remembering what it was like to meditate on this station. Which emotions were dominant? What aspect of the experience stands out for you now?

Imagine
"Condemned by the Sanhedrin"

Their voices emerge out of darkness. The scent of wine and vinegar. You stand before them. They pant like hungry dogs. No humor. No irony. Circles of shadow frame their disjointed faces, a room of cracked mirrors, fearful men reflected a thousand times. Dark halos, their lips twisted like those who speak from both sides of their mouths. They talk of revolution. They talk of peace. They know nothing. The same angel of the desert who did this to Pharaoh is whispering in their ears tonight: *Harden your hearts.* There is nothing that can be said. No truth. This is all just motions. A mock trial. Conspiracy of cowards. They feud among themselves.

Their anger is so boring.

They tear down what God created.

You will rebuild.

A Conversation with
God the Father

A colloquy is a one-on-one conversation between you and God, Jesus, Mary, a saint, or an angel. It's an opportunity for you to speak from the heart in words and emotions you use every day. If you're feeling anxious or worried, tell God about it. If you're elated and filled with dreams of the future, then share those with God. Don't hold back. Let loose the way you would with a trusted friend.

Imagine God is with you in a beautiful garden of lavender, hyacinth, and roses. It is evening. You smell the flowers and the brine of the distant sea. You hear a commotion, and in the distance you watch soldiers arrest Jesus. You begin speaking to God: "Don't let this happen. How can you allow this? Do something." You tremble and think, *If you can let this happen to Jesus, will you let this happen to me?*

How does God respond? Reflect on those answers and then ask, "What am I doing for Christ? What can I do for Christ? How can I help him?"

Speak your answers to God. If words do not come, just remain present in that silence.

The Fourth Station: Jesus Is Denied by Peter

Now Peter was sitting outside in the courtyard. A servant-girl came to him and said, "You also were with Jesus the Galilean." But he denied it before all of them, saying, "I do not know what you are talking about." When he went out to the porch, another servant-girl saw him, and she said to the bystanders, "This man was with Jesus of Nazareth." Again he denied it with an oath, "I do not know the man." After a little while the bystanders came up and said to Peter, "Certainly you are also one of them, for your accent betrays you." Then he began to curse, and he swore an oath, "I do not know the man!" At that moment the cock crowed. Then Peter remembered what Jesus had said: "Before the cock crows, you will deny me three times." And he went out and wept bitterly.
—Matthew 26:69–75

Jesus' Response: He Accepts
Others' Weaknesses

Over the years, I've always thought that Judas got a bum rap. Yes, he sold his friend down the river for money. Of course, that friend happened to be God Incarnate. Big mistake, Jude. For the medieval poet Dante, that would buy you a first-class ticket to hell, and not to the warm circles but to the burning icy part.

Yet, look at Peter. The guy acts like a numbskull. He's just like all of us, which may be why I love him so much. He can talk a big game: "Yeah, Jesus, I'm with you all the way, man! Don't worry about anything. I got your back." But when the moment of truth arrives, he folds like me playing poker with my kids (my kids are little card sharks). Judas betrays Jesus once. Granted, it's a big once that leads to his crucifixion. But Peter? Peter betrays Jesus three times! After the first encounter, he has a couple of chances to redeem himself, but his fear gets the better of him, and by the time that famous cock crows, Peter has sunk deeper than he did when he lost faith during his attempt to walk on water.

Jesus is absent in this station, yet we know that he still loves Peter—so much that he makes Peter the foundation of the church. If *gospel* means "good news," then some of the good news is that God loves losers. (The joke, of course, is that God *has* to love losers, because he created so many of them.) Regardless of our flaws, God still loves us.

Think of some of the cornerstones of our faith—huge losers because they were murderers! Moses murdered an Egyptian soldier. David ordered a hit on Uriah, one of his loyal soldiers. Paul enjoyed pesecuting followers of Jesus and stood around as Stephen was stoned to death.

Yet we know that, regardless of who they were or what they did, God still loved these deeply flawed and sinful men. This doesn't make their crimes any less serious, but it demonstrates the extent of God's forgiveness for those who make tragic mistakes.

If Jesus can love those who betray him, can't we love all those people who, at times, seem so unlovable? Can't we forgive a friend for his imperfections and accept him for who he is? Can't we love someone who may not have the capacity to love us back? We can respond this way without becoming victims. Bad behavior should never be tolerated, but love and forgiveness are ways of releasing chains of frustration, pain, and sadness that entangle us and keep us from growing closer not only to the people around us but also to God.

Encountering Jesus

Imagine it's a cold spring night. Your best friend has been taken away, arrested, and you fear that you might be next. As you try to lie low, a number of people recognize you as a follower of the man who was arrested. You have committed no crime, unless friendship is a crime. So what do you do when people accuse you of being associated with him? What is your response?

Have you ever betrayed a friend or felt the need to disassociate yourself from someone who was having a tough time? Why did you do this? What are your feelings about your actions? If you were in the same situation now, would you do anything differently?

Do you accept the flaws in your family and friends? Is there something that prevents you from fully loving someone who may have made mistakes in the past?

Take These Words to Prayer

Then Peter came and said to him, "Lord, if another member of the church sins against me, how often should I forgive? As many as seven times?" Jesus said to him, "Not seven times, but, I tell you, seventy-seven times."

—Matthew 18:21–22

Review This Experience

Later today, or even tomorrow, spend a few quiet moments remembering what it was like to meditate on this station. Which emotions were dominant? What aspect of the experience stands out for you now?

Imagine
"Denied by Peter"

You loved him before you knew him. He, fashioned for loyalty, was always by your side. It was hard to get rid of him. Both of you would rise in the mornings before the cock crowed and walk the hills before dawn, watching the sun rise over this land of tombs. Together, you would remember the cloudless evenings passing the portico, the overturned boats docked for the night. Then, the flutter of noisy birds.

An omen, you said.

Of what? he asked.

In time.

The two of you would talk for hours. When you needed to be alone, he wouldn't leave. *You must go.*

I won't leave you.

Now, black winds. Night has fallen. Your hands are cold. Your heart is sleepless. You wait, knowing he won't come.

In the distance, the crowing of early dawn.

The Fifth Station: Jesus Is Judged by Pilate

Now at the festival the governor was accustomed to release a prisoner for the crowd, anyone whom they wanted. At that time they had a notorious prisoner, called Jesus Barabbas. So after they had gathered, Pilate said to them, "Whom do you want me to release for you, Jesus Barabbas or Jesus who is called the Messiah?" For he realized that it was out of jealousy that they had handed him over. While he was sitting on the judgment seat, his wife sent word to him, "Have nothing to do with that innocent man, for today I have suffered a great deal because of a dream about him." Now the chief priests and the elders persuaded the crowds to ask for Barabbas and to have Jesus killed. The governor again said to them, "Which of the two do you want me to release for you?" And they said, "Barabbas." Pilate said to them, "Then what should I do with Jesus who is called the Messiah?" All of them said, "Let him be crucified!" Then he asked, "Why, what evil has he

done?" But they shouted all the more, "Let him be crucified!" So when Pilate saw that he could do nothing, but rather that a riot was beginning, he took some water and washed his hands before the crowd, saying, "I am innocent of this man's blood; see to it yourselves."
—Matthew 27:15–24

Jesus' Response: He Is Quiet

In this station, we do not see or hear Jesus; he is offstage. Yet he is the object of a spectacle, humiliated before yet another crowd, for being who he is. Here is a man who was preaching love, forgiveness, kindness, and mercy—and this crowd wants him dead.

Imagine yourself vulnerable, standing before a group of people who loved you a couple of days ago and now are out for blood. The ebb and flow of public opinion! Try to be Jesus' eyes and ears, and look out at the sea of people, all of them hating you and passing judgment. This crowd knows that by choosing Barabbas, they send Jesus to his death.

It's important to notice what we don't see in this particular station. We don't see Jesus objecting. We don't see Jesus snarling or yelling. He is not arguing with Pilate or the bloodthirsty crowd. He is instead quiet, accepting, and dignified.

Some years back, a coworker of mine named Joan was diagnosed with cancer. She was a woman of great faith, and though she was much older than I, by maybe forty years, we had a bond that was very special. She had taken a job in a publishing house, but she was still a part-time actress and had appeared in numerous commercials during her career. What

I admired so much about Joan was that, even though acting was her passion, when she was at work in our editorial offices, she was at work. She was focused, professional, and astute. An all-around class act.

I'm not sure how many of our coworkers knew she had cancer. Joan was quiet in everything she did, though inside her body were raging crowds of cancerous cells. Sometimes she would tell me about her doctor's appointments, and I would watch her frail hand gently touch a small crucifix she wore around her neck. Though her treatments were painful and left her exhausted, she still came in to work every day and did her job with poise and dedication.

That is, until she didn't come in to work. In the end, none of us knew just how sick Joan had become. One evening she went home after work, and I never saw her again. She passed away in her sleep.

Like Jesus, Joan lived courageously in the face of difficult odds. Like Jesus as he stood before his accusers, she never protested. Instead, she carried her cross quietly and with great dignity.

Encountering Jesus

Imagine you are a Roman soldier standing near Pilate. You look upon Jesus, can see his face, his eyes, his ragged hair. He looks exhausted. You then look at Pilate. He's a strong and important man, has been well fed for a long time with the best foods and wine. Does Jesus make eye contact with him? Is Pilate putting on a show for the crowd? Is he sincere in his words and actions or just a politician playing to a crowd? Allow your eyes to walk around the room. Look outside. What do you hear? Can you smell the sweat of the day? Is the sun bright, or are dark clouds forming? As a soldier, you are loyal to Caesar, but you've heard this man preach about love and charity. How do you feel as the crowd cheers for Barabbas?

Seek out an image of the painting called *Ecce Homo*, which means "behold the man," by Antonio Ciseri. Gaze upon this depiction of Jesus before Pilate. The politician's hand is pointed right at the heart of the prisoner. There are witnesses on the left. A group of women are looking away with closed mouths, holding on to each other for support. What do you make of Jesus' posture? What is going on in his mind as he stands there, a spectacle?

Take These Words to Prayer

He said, "Go out and stand on the mountain before the Lord, for the Lord is about to pass by." Now there was a great wind, so strong that it was splitting mountains and breaking rocks in pieces before the Lord, but the Lord was not in the wind; and after the wind an earthquake, but the Lord was not in the earthquake; and after the earthquake a fire, but the Lord was not in the fire; and after the fire a sound of sheer silence.

—1 Kings 19:11–12

Review This Experience

Later today, or even tomorrow, spend a few quiet moments remembering what it was like to meditate on this station. Which emotions were dominant? What aspect of the experience stands out for you now?

Imagine
"Judged by Pilate"

I thought he would be taller, but he is just a man. Let it be done.

The Sixth Station:
Jesus Is Scourged and
Crowned with Thorns

Then the soldiers of the governor took Jesus into the governor's headquarters, and they gathered the whole cohort around him. They stripped him and put a scarlet robe on him, and after twisting some thorns into a crown, they put it on his head. They put a reed in his right hand and knelt before him and mocked him, saying, "Hail, King of the Jews!" They spat on him, and took the reed and struck him on the head.
—Matthew 27:27–30

Jesus' Response: He Is Broken

I remember the first time my oldest son cut himself. He was a year and a half old. We were in the backyard. It was summertime and he was wearing blue shorts. Still wobbly on his legs, he fell and scraped his knee. He didn't cry. But I did. Not because it was a serious injury but because, as I watched the blood form on his skin, I realized that this was the first time his skin had been opened, that this was the first of many scrapes and cuts that he would suffer, as we all do. And he would suffer not just physically but also mentally and emotionally in the disappointments, losses, and challenges all of us encounter on earth.

Here, at this station, we see Jesus' body broken. This has always been a difficult passage for me to read. Jesus is an innocent man who is just trying to remind people to put God first, to be merciful—and for that his flesh is torn apart. He has not raised a sword or a hand against anyone, and yet the soldiers raise theirs against him. Jesus doesn't fight back. He takes his punishment and stands strong against his attackers even as his body is being torn to pieces.

It can be easy to ignore just how painful this was for Jesus. As much as we can empathize with someone, we can never really know another's pain. There's just no way for us to switch bodies to experience it. But, just for a moment, imagine the last time you got a paper cut. This might sound ridiculous, but those things hurt! A bad paper cut can redirect a lot of your energies throughout the rest of the day. So if something like that hurts, imagine what it must have felt like for Jesus to be flogged and to have thorns pressed into his scalp.

Jesus is broken. He anticipated this with the breaking of the bread at the Last Supper. As he split the loaf in half to share with his friends, he offered a prediction of what was to come the following day.

There is something unique about pain. For many of us, it inspires generosity. I don't mean that in a positive sense. When we are suffering, many of us want to share that suffering with others, not by expressing our feelings in a constructive way but by trying to make others feel as miserable as we do. Have you ever had a bad day at work and then later that day snapped at a friend, or a spouse, a child, or even a stranger at the store? When many of us experience intense pain, we just can't handle it. We have to give it away, and we do that by inflicting pain on others. We may be the cheapest people in the world, who hoard everything, but when it comes to pain, we give it away freely. "I don't want this feeling, so I'm going to give some to you," we say.

This isn't to say that we shouldn't share our pain with a trusted friend or a counselor. There is something about pain that we need to deal with. All the repressed pain that builds and builds and builds, that we never deal with in a mature, organized way, leads to disaster.

Terrorism, mass shootings, child abuse, war—all of these evils stem from brokenness, which then leads to an unbroken cycle of pain. The only way to stop the cycle is to break it. This feels like an impossible task. But it can be done, through acts of mercy, prayer, counseling, love, friendship, and by making the decision—really deciding—that this has to end *now*.

Jesus, the bread of life, is broken here. Yet there is no eye for an eye. He will not seek vengeance. Instead, he acts like a sponge, absorbing all the violence and hatred. In turn he will convert all that negative energy, all that waste, into something positive.

God's love may have been the fuel for Jesus' resurrection, but it was the flame of human hatred that set this miracle ablaze.

Encountering Jesus

Imagine that you are Jesus being led into a yard, where you see instruments of torture: knives, clubs, and whips. You have been a preacher of peace. Now you stand before men who have the authority to harm you. One of the soldiers fastens you to a post so you cannot escape. It's hard to breathe. Then you feel the flesh on your back being torn open as another soldier unleashes a whip. What do you hear? What do you feel? What do you taste in your mouth? Are you afraid? Angry? Despairing? Do you call out to God for help? Are you asking God why this is happening?

Disappointment, abuse, poverty, bullying—all of these leave us spiritually broken. Recall some situations in which you've experienced the most pain. On a piece of paper, write out all your insecurities and doubts, all the suffering you've experienced in your life, all the places you've been torn. Then imagine placing that list into the hands of Jesus and asking him to help you to convert these earthly experiences into something heavenly.

Take These Words to Prayer

But even if you do suffer for doing what is right, you are blessed. Do not fear what they fear, and do not be intimidated, but in your hearts sanctify Christ as Lord.

—1 Peter 3:14–15

Review This Experience

Later today, or even tomorrow, spend a few quiet moments remembering what it was like to meditate on this station. Which emotions were dominant? What aspect of the experience stands out for you now?

Imagine
"Scourged"

He stands over you, a hollow man in hollow armor. He is the same age as you. You stare at his empty eyes.

You have no power except what has been given to you by the Father.

Lashes on your back like birds screaming. Blood runs from the corners of your mouth. His blows burn like a bush on fire. He breaks your nose. Hands raised, you look to the sky and close your eyes, trying not to hear the thunder.

The crowning. The sovereignty of pain. Blood from his dirty fingers mixes with yours. You are now brethren as he raises you to your feet in a devil's embrace.

As boys, you didn't know each other, but you both looked at the same stars and in the summertime prayed for rain.

The Seventh Station:
Jesus Bears the Cross

After mocking him, they stripped him of the robe and put his own clothes on him. Then they led him away to crucify him.
—Matthew 27:31

Jesus' Response: He Endures

Even after all the abuse Jesus suffers, he does not give up. Though he will struggle and become weaker as he makes his journey through the streets of Jerusalem, there is a strength that allows him to pick up his cross and carry his burden.

External pain is easy to understand. It arises if someone strikes us, if we fall and injure ourselves, or if we get sick. However, internal pain—mental, emotional, psychological, and spiritual—arises whenever we challenge God's will. This can be very tricky. We are not robots; we experience fear, sadness, doubt, and regret whenever a situation around us changes for the worse. All is fine while there's food on the table, but not so much when the cupboard is bare. Life is great when the job is secure, but not so great when the company goes through a restructuring that could lead to job loss. We don't want these uncertain conditions. We want things to be different.

In the Stations of the Cross, when do we first see Jesus begin to suffer? In the garden. Why? Because he's anticipating the events that are about to unfold—when he challenges, albeit briefly, God's will. He wants to try to avoid the future if he can, but he quickly realizes that it's not his will that's important but God's will. God never said that we won't experience pain or abuse or suffering. All the saints suffered, but we honor these people because through it all, they drew strength in their faith by surrendering to Divine Providence.

This can be so difficult to do and difficult to accept, especially when it comes to illness, loss of a loved one, or the consequences of others' actions. There are moments when we're tempted to give up, when the voice inside our head says, "This is not fair. You can't do it. There's no reason to keep on fighting. Just give up." Yet we have access to this supernatural power of endurance.

Whatever you're going through is probably not fair. There is no retreat from life or the chaos that ensues from the sometimes terrible and demeaning actions of others. And while we are asked to surrender to God's will, there is no surrender in *this* world until our final moment. That doesn't mean we can't rest, catch our breath, or even escape our burdens from time to time, but as Thomas Merton wrote, "The more you try to avoid suffering, the more you suffer, because smaller and more insignificant things begin to torture you, in proportion to your fear of being hurt. The one who does most to avoid suffering is, in the end, the one who suffers most."

For many years, when my wife was a teacher's assistant, we attended the Special Olympics, a sporting event for children and adults with intellectual disabilities. I recommend that anyone who feels that he or she is having a bad day watch one of these competitions. Here are children living with genetic diseases, cerebral palsy, mental retardation, and autism, pushing themselves through their debilitating physical and intellectual conditions.

One year, a teenage girl with misshapen legs competed in a footrace. As she left the starting line, she stumbled and hit the ground. The crowd winced, but she didn't stay down. She picked herself up and ran. Then quickly fell down. Got up. Ran some more. And fell again. Hard. But something happened on that last fall. She somehow found a focus inside her that maybe wasn't there at the start of the race. You could see her face change, her eyes locking on that finish line. She didn't fall again, and even though she came in last, and even though it must have been painful for her parents to watch their young girl fall so many times, she endured. And she had the biggest smile on her face when she crossed that finish line.

We can draw from that well of the Spirit too, and as you meditate and pray on this station, ask God to help you accept God's will and remind you that you have been given the ability to meet any challenge, to face your fear, to rise and walk.

Encountering Jesus

Imagine yourself as a young girl or boy staring out a window. Below you are the dusty streets of an ancient city. The air is warm. You listen to loud voices and commotion. You look down and see two soldiers placing a heavy wooden beam on a bloodied man. What do you feel? What are the people on the street doing? What are they saying? Are they mocking the man? Is anyone protesting? You watch the man, dazed and disoriented, slowly make his way to a place you know is a hill of execution. What strikes you as you watch the scene unfold?

Think of a time when you wanted to give up but didn't. How did you get through that period in your life? Where did your strength come from? Recall another time, when you did give up, a moment that still weighs heavily on your mind. Talk to God about your decision. Were you frightened, angry, confused by the events at the time? Did you walk away from something? Bring this event before God and ask for help in sorting out your feelings and regrets.

Take These Words to Prayer

I can do all things through him who strengthens me.

—Philippians 4:13

Review This Experience

Later today, or even tomorrow, spend a few quiet moments remembering what it was like to meditate on this station. Which emotions were dominant? What aspect of the experience stands out for you now?

Imagine
"Bears the Cross"

Bruised skin. Purple fingers. Dust coats your mouth. Heavy air hangs on you like another layer of skin. At noon the sun casts hardly a shadow.

This wood is so heavy. How can wood be this heavy? A voice. Not just one voice. Countless. The unfaithful. The murderers. The liars. The lukewarm. The poor. The sick. The lonely. They are all in your head, all on your back. So many. How is this possible?

Your shoulders burn, and you remember a girl walking in the cool breeze of a summer morning. She vanished from sight, leaving behind the smell of lavender. She has returned. Follow her now. She knows where to take you. Follow her. Follow her.

A Conversation with Mary, Jesus' Mother

Imagine you are holding Mary's hand as she follows Jesus along the way to his crucifixion. The air is stale and warm, but her hand is cool. She is crying, but she keeps pace with her son, never taking her eyes off him. As you make your way with her to Golgotha, she whispers something in your ear. What does she say? What do you say to her? How can you help her as she watches her son being treated so brutally?

In a similar way, how can you keep your eyes always on Jesus? What can you do for Mary to help her help others? How can you work together for the benefit of Jesus?

As you hold Mary's hand, speak to her about whatever you are feeling, knowing that she is always with her son and in turn is keeping pace with you every day.

The Eighth Station: Jesus Is Helped by Simon of Cyrene

As they went out, they came upon a man from Cyrene named Simon; they compelled this man to carry his cross.
—Matthew 27:32

Jesus' Response: He Allows Others to Help

Sometimes our problems become too much to handle. Even for Jesus, though he was God, his body was still susceptible to pain, sunburn, dehydration, and exhaustion. Like any human being, he needed time to sleep, to be alone, and to rest. In this station, Jesus is in a most extreme situation. With his body battered and exposed, he needs help bearing his burden.

And so we need to remember that we can't always make it on our own. That we need companions, helpers, support from others. Be accepting of this. Accept when the burden becomes too much to bear. Allow others to help you. Sometimes, by offering help, others have an opportunity for their own transformation.

We don't know much about Simon of Cyrene, and he's mostly neglected as a character in films and works of fiction that are based on the Passion story. Was he a willing or reluctant volunteer? Was his act one of mercy, or did he fear the Roman soldiers who ordered it? What do you think happened to him after he heard the news of Jesus' resurrection? Did it change his life?

Simon's name comes from a Hebrew phrase meaning "he has heard." What has Simon heard? The call. The call for all of us to help lessen the burden of others. The Cyrenian movement, popular in the United Kingdom, is a group of volunteers who look to alleviate suffering around them, to help the homeless and disenfranchised. These people lend a helping hand because they, as their name from Simon of Cyrene suggests, have heard the call of those in need.

Do we? Do we hear the call?

Encountering Jesus

Imagine you are Simon of Cyrene. You are standing around watching yet another man being led to execution, only this one is in pretty bad shape. A soldier grabs you and orders you to help this prisoner, who can barely stand. You pick up the man's cross; it's heavier than anything you've ever carried. What do you feel? What do you say to the dazed man walking next to you? Does he answer? What does he say to you?

Is there someone in your family, community, parish, or neighborhood who is suffering physically, emotionally, or financially? Maybe this person is hungry or in need of a simple act of kindness or encouragement. What can you do to help that person persevere through tough times? How can you help a loved one, a stranger, or a coworker carry his or her burden?

Take These Words to Prayer

Men are beginning to realize that they are not individuals but persons in society, that man alone is weak and adrift, that he must seek strength in common action.

—Dorothy Day

Review This Experience

Later today, or even tomorrow, spend a few quiet moments remembering what it was like to meditate on this station. Which emotions were dominant? What aspect of the experience stands out for you now?

Imagine
"Helped by Simon"

Dogs sniff blood on the streets. You fall. A soldier strikes your leg. You cannot move. The weight is too much. All this bothers the man with the boyish face, who looks on as if looking into the eyes of demons. A soldier seizes him.

Carry this.

He picks up the heavy wood. Struggles, but bears the weight. You look into his eyes. The color of desert sand. You think of water but know you cannot drink.

The Ninth Station: Jesus Meets the Women of Jerusalem

A great number of the people followed him, and among them were women who were beating their breasts and wailing for him. But Jesus turned to them and said, "Daughters of Jerusalem, do not weep for me, but weep for yourselves and for your children. For the days are surely coming when they will say, 'Blessed are the barren, and the wombs that never bore, and the breasts that never nursed.' Then they will begin to say to the mountains, 'Fall on us'; and to the hills, 'Cover us.' For if they do this when the wood is green, what will happen when it is dry?"
—Luke 23:27–31

Jesus' Response: He Thinks of Others

Even in the midst of his own pain and suffering, Jesus is not thinking about himself. From the start he has been God-centered, other-centered. He is the embodiment of the golden rule, which asks that we love God and love our neighbors as ourselves. When, in the ninth station, Jesus meets the women of Jerusalem, he has the chance to tell them how unfairly he has been treated, that a friend betrayed him and that the charges against him are false—all things that are true. If he chooses, he can encourage those around him to revolt against the Romans.

Of course, Jesus doesn't do any of those things. Instead, he turns his attention to others and says, "Don't cry for me . . . cry for yourselves."

These are unsettling words, and at first blush they may sound like the words of a man seeking vengeance. But that's not what he's doing.

Jesus is many things: the Son of God, the son of a carpenter, a rabbi, a teacher. He is also a prophet, and we see here that Jesus uses his prophetic vision to warn others about the repercussions that will follow if we live our lives as if God were not present. God is ever with us. Yet, with the exception of Jesus' mother and the demons who feared him, most people could not see God before their eyes. Jesus seems to be saying here, "This is how society treats God? With mockery and abuse?" Those actions will have repercussions.

This isn't a threat. This is reality. If we toss a bowling ball out a window, it will fall to the earth and crash through a windshield. Gravity is a law of our space and time. If you want to break that law, then you'll have to suffer the consequences.

The same holds true when it comes to heavenly matters. Are you living as if God weren't present in the here and now? Are you acting as if God isn't important? If you reject God, then there will be an aftermath. This isn't a threat. This isn't retribution. It is simple cause and effect.

Encountering Jesus

Imagine the face of Jesus as he makes his way toward Calvary. Imagine you are one of the women of Jerusalem. Through your tears, look into his eyes. What do you see? What does his voice sound like? Is it strong, or is he struggling to speak? If you could help this man, what would you do? When he speaks, how do you interpret his words? Do they shock you? Scare you?

Think back to a time when you were struggling through a problem, but instead of focusing on yourself, you directed your attention to someone else in need. Maybe you were on a tight deadline, or nervous about doing your job correctly, when a coworker came looking to help, but you could tell that she was distraught about something herself. How did God move through you?

Take These Words to Prayer

Jesus came to Galilee, proclaiming the good news of God, and saying, "The time is fulfilled, and the kingdom of God has come near; repent, and believe in the good news."

—Mark 1:14–15

Review This Experience

Later today, or even tomorrow, spend a few quiet moments remembering what it was like to meditate on this station. Which emotions were dominant? What aspect of the experience stands out for you now?

Imagine
"The Women of Jerusalem"

This crowded street. You see them through matted hair. They squawk like blackbirds, thirteen of them, weeping, anxious voices, performing a dance to ease you into the next life.

"Don't cry for me," you say. "The world keeps God away. Weep because of that."

The Tenth Station:
Jesus Is Crucified

And when they came to a place called Golgotha (which means Place of a Skull), they offered him wine to drink, mixed with gall; but when he tasted it, he would not drink it. And when they had crucified him, they divided his clothes among themselves by casting lots; then they sat down there and kept watch over him.
—Matthew 27:33–36

Jesus' Response: He Feels Pain

How often do we turn to an aspirin or some bourbon or chocolate when we have pain or anxiety? Fortunately, those of us in the Western world do not have to suffer crucifixion (people in some parts of the world have become reacquainted with it), but everyone has to face daily problems and burdens. Maybe, at the end of a long day, we like to throw back a couple of drinks, vegetate in front of the TV, or down a couple of cupcakes just as a way of decompressing and releasing tension.

These examples seem trite in contrast to the scene we witness in this station. Yet, essentially, in taking these little actions, we are trying to assuage pain or fill a void. We stress-eat, or stress-drink or stress-smoke. These things are supposed to take the edge off, and they do temporarily, but once the effects of whatever it is that we've taken inside of us wear off, we are still left with our problems, our depression, our sadness, and our pain.

There are theological reasons Jesus refuses to drink wine here, but if we look at this objectively, we see that Jesus doesn't want to numb his pain. He fully embraces the situation he's in. He didn't try to run away earlier, and he won't run away now by taking a drink mixed with myrrh, which has narcotic qualities, to dull the pain. Some may call this masochistic, but maybe that's just because we've become a society that likes to solve problems instantly instead of allowing ourselves to feel fully our discomfort.

I'm not saying you can't just veg out every once in a while, but are there times in our lives when we are numbing a pain that we need to feel to help us grow in character? Those experiences of discomfort, emptiness, and desolation can sometimes be the place where God is most present.

Encountering Jesus

Imagine that you are Jesus. Soldiers lay you on the ground and drive heavy spikes through your skin. The pain is unbearable, and as you cry out in agony, you notice a slight breeze blow over your face. In your fear, in your anguish, that breeze reminds you of God's presence. What do you say to God as you're suffering? What do you say to God as the soldiers lift the cross and expose you to the world?

Place yourself in God's presence by becoming as quiet as you can, then reflect on your life and on whether there have been times when you avoided a responsibility or tried to dull a pain. Ask God to help illuminate that moment for you. What was the underlying cause of your actions? Bring this to prayer and ask God for advice and guidance.

Take These Words to Prayer

Reread the Scripture passage, Matthew 27:33–36, that opens this chapter. What about it resonates most with you? Is there an image or a word that has particular meaning? Pray on that word or image, asking God to draw you into a deeper awareness of his presence.

Review This Experience

Later today, or even tomorrow, spend a few quiet moments remembering what it was like to meditate on this station. Which emotions were dominant? What aspect of the experience stands out for you now?

Imagine
"Crucified"

As a boy you would play in places like this, with the cracked earth and arthritic-looking rocks. An old man, a collector of bones, would pulverize the dead, mixing the meal with oil and malachite to paint astrological charts on the skins of lambs. He told you that one day you would become a king. It was written in the stars, he said. You stood fixed, looking at his cart of curiosities, balls of crystal, amulets like eyes, butterflies pinned to bits of cypress.

Now you see traces of clouds. A knife, a rope, nails, and a hammer. You used these tools in your father's workshop, joining wood together. Now, a crude carpenter joins you to a beam.

When the iron pierces your flesh, you think of a dove descending from the sky, whispering something in your ear. The promise of honey, olives, milk. The promise of love.

A Conversation with Jesus on the Cross

Imagine Christ our Lord suspended on the cross before you and converse with him. How is it that he, although he is Creator, has come to make himself a human being? How is it that he has passed from eternal life to death here in time? How is it that he has died in this way for our sins?

In a similar way, reflect on your own life and ask, "What have I done for Christ? What am I doing for Christ? What ought I to do for Christ?"

In this way, too, gazing on him in so pitiful a state as he hangs on the cross, speak out whatever comes to your mind.

—Adapted from *The Spiritual Exercises*, 53

The Eleventh Station:
Jesus Promises His Kingdom to the Good Thief

Two others also, who were criminals, were led away to be put to death with him. When they came to the place that is called The Skull, they crucified Jesus there with the criminals, one on his right and one on his left. Then Jesus said, "Father, forgive them; for they do not know what they are doing." And they cast lots to divide his clothing. And the people stood by, watching; but the leaders scoffed at him, saying, "He saved others; let him save himself if he is the Messiah of God, his chosen one!" The soldiers also mocked him, coming up and offering him sour wine, and saying, "If you are the King of the Jews, save yourself!" There was also an inscription over him, "This is the King of the Jews."
One of the criminals who were hanged there kept deriding him and saying, "Are you not the Messiah? Save yourself and us!" But the other rebuked him,

saying, "Do you not fear God, since you are under the same sentence of condemnation? And we indeed have been condemned justly, for we are getting what we deserve for our deeds, but this man has done nothing wrong." Then he said, "Jesus, remember me when you come into your kingdom." He replied, "Truly I tell you, today you will be with me in Paradise."
—Luke 23:32–43

Jesus' Response: He Forgives

Torn flesh from flogging. Thorns piercing skin. Nails driven through hands and feet. Exposure to the sun. Bodies hanging like rotting meat.

In the midst of all this physical and psychological pain, how does Jesus react? The temptation to curse everyone around him, to give his pain away by threatening the soldiers or shaming the followers who abandoned him, must have been real. It would have been easy to condemn, to judge. Instead, Jesus offers mercy: "Father, forgive them; for they do not know what they are doing."

Jesus' resurrection is *the* supernatural event that changes history. Things are never the same after Jesus rises to new life. Although God forgives throughout the Bible, to see Jesus offer forgiveness after all the trials and tribulations he has been through is a moment that destroys the Old Covenant idea of an eye for an eye. This act of forgiveness, this act of compassion during a time of ultimate struggle, sets in motion the new standard for what it means to be a true human being. No longer are we flawed creations who live to seek revenge on those who wrong us. No, Jesus' actions say, there is a new ideal, one grounded in love and nonviolence.

But even after Jesus' sacrifice, and even after his resurrection, sin, pain, despair, and confusion remain in the world. Why? Shouldn't they have been eradicated with these acts of Jesus? As Thomas Merton wrote, "God has left sin in the world in order that there may be forgiveness; not only the secret forgiveness by which He Himself cleanses our souls, but the manifest forgiveness by which we have mercy on one another and so give expression to the fact that He is living, by His mercy, in our own hearts."

Maybe this is why so many of us feel overwhelmed emotionally when we encounter Jesus on the cross. That stirring, that longing in our souls—*that* is God's mercy and forgiveness beating inside us.

Encountering Jesus

Imagine you are a criminal being crucified with Jesus. Try to imagine the pain in your hands, your back, your head, your feet, and your legs. You cry out in agony to the man hanging next to you. He offers you mercy and the hope of a new life. What do you say to him?

Think back to a time when someone extended forgiveness to you. How did this action change you? Are there people you need to forgive? Make a list. Then, stop reading this and go forgive them.

Take These Words to Prayer

This is my blood of the covenant, which is poured out for many for the forgiveness of sins.

—Matthew 26:28

Review This Experience

Later today, or even tomorrow, spend a few quiet moments remembering what it was like to meditate on this station. Which emotions were dominant? What aspect of the experience stands out for you now?

Imagine
"Promise to a Thief"

You look into his eyes. You never had a son, but you wish now you could be a father to this man. He was unexpected. You thought you were journeying alone, didn't expect this man to be your companion into the next life.

God of surprises. God of mercy.

My son, today we travel light.

The Twelfth Station: Jesus Speaks to His Mother and the Disciple

Meanwhile, standing near the cross of Jesus were his mother, and his mother's sister, Mary the wife of Clopas, and Mary Magdalene. When Jesus saw his mother and the disciple whom he loved standing beside her, he said to his mother, "Woman, here is your son." Then he said to the disciple, "Here is your mother." And from that hour the disciple took her into his own home.
—John 19:25–27

Jesus' Response: He Watches
Over His Family

A son suffering before his mother, a man dying before his friend's eyes. Although the focus of the Stations is on Jesus, we can turn for a moment to Mary and Mary Magdalene. Here the two most important women in his life are at the foot of the cross, holding vigil. Along with them is the beloved disciple whom tradition holds to be John. They are the only three of Jesus' companions who are left; all others have fled. This holy trinity keeps watch over this man they all love.

These are Jesus' last moments. His work is just about complete, but he needs to bind a relationship here on the earth so that it is forever bound in heaven.

Jesus places his attention on family, on relationship. Again, he's thinking not about himself but about taking care of his family. In first-century Palestine (and in many cultures even today), a son must take care of his mother after his father has died. We don't know how long Jesus' father Joseph has been gone, but we can imagine that Jesus was providing for Mary after his father's passing. As each breath Jesus takes leads him closer to death, he knows his mother will become vulnerable. He wants to protect his mother and so unites her with one of his best friends so that John and Mary can become a new family on earth. Jesus, even as he is dying, is embodying the fourth commandment: to honor his mother, Mary, and his father, God.

Jesus' actions reveal his deep commitment to others. His final act of mercy is directed toward his mother, to protect her, to care for her, to provide for her in his absence. If this is Jesus' wish, then it is our obligation not only to offer this kind of love to our families but also to uphold Mary, the Blessed Mother, in our lives as well.

Encountering Jesus

Imagine that you are the Blessed Mother. You remember the day your son was born, the pain you experienced in childbirth, your baby's first cry. And now you are present as your son nears his final cry in life. What are you experiencing as you look upon your son while he hangs in tatters on the cross?

Now, in the present, how can you make daily changes to honor and uphold your family? Regardless of past hurts, how can you make a daily commitment to help your family grow in love and trust?

Take These Words to Prayer

And the child's father and mother were amazed at what was being said about him. Then Simeon blessed them and said to his mother Mary, "This child is destined for the falling and the rising of many in Israel, and to be a sign that will be opposed so that the inner thoughts of many will be revealed—and a sword will pierce your own soul too."

—Luke 2:33–35

Review This Experience

Later today, or even tomorrow, spend a few quiet moments remembering what it was like to meditate on this station. Which emotions were dominant? What aspect of the experience stands out for you now?

Imagine
"Mother, Brother"

You are a boy. You remember the dark room and hissing like steam from a kettle. You could not see it. But you could feel it, moving over the floor, inching closer. You knew you were going to die. But then an open door, a bright light, and she struck, crushing the asp's head with her foot. The snake's tail flashed back and forth. Your mother, panting, said, "This will be the first of many."

You look upon her now, mother of your heart, crusher of serpents. She holds her hands aloft, asking God to deliver you back into her arms. Soon she will hold you; soon you will feel her embrace. But now, bless her, and give her to another. She is no longer yours; she belongs to everyone.

The Thirteenth Station:
Jesus Dies on the Cross

From noon on, darkness came over the whole land until three in the afternoon. And about three o'clock Jesus cried with a loud voice, "Eli, Eli, lema sabachthani?" that is, "My God, my God, why have you forsaken me?" When some of the bystanders heard it, they said, "This man is calling for Elijah." At once one of them ran and got a sponge, filled it with sour wine, put it on a stick, and gave it to him to drink. But the others said, "Wait, let us see whether Elijah will come to save him."
Then Jesus cried again with a loud voice and breathed his last.
—Matthew 27:45–50

Jesus' Response: He Weeps

So far, along the Way of the Cross, Jesus has acted like a superhero, a silent tough guy. A first-century Clint Eastwood in a robe, taking his shots and accepting everything that comes his way.

But as we reach this station, the pain and sorrow have become too much for Jesus to bear. He cries out to God. For hundreds of years theologians have debated whether in saying these words Jesus actually felt abandoned by God or was invoking Psalm 22 as a form of prayer and a declaration of hope. But all we really know is that a final wave of emotion in Jesus breaks through.

It can be difficult to express emotions, especially if we've suffered great pain. Yet in this journey to the cross, we see that Jesus has endured great suffering—not just the pain of body and mind but also the deep supernatural pain given to him by God, the burden of all our sins, the agony of accepting all the collective lies, killings, betrayals, and deceits that are part of human life. The loneliness and the depravity are too much for even God to bear, and we hear Jesus cry out and give up his life.

Don't bury the pain. Lament. Cry out. Doing so leads to new life.

Encountering Jesus

Imagine you are on the cross. Imagine that all the pain that millions of people have inflicted on one another is now on your shoulders, pushing you down, suffocating you. What do you see as the world around you starts to darken? What are you experiencing in your last breaths?

Meditate on the words "My God, my God." What do these words mean to you? Do you think Jesus is forsaken on the cross?

Take These Words to Prayer

I abandon myself entirely to you; enlighten me, lead me, uphold me, take possession of me.

—*Abandonment to Divine Providence*

Review This Experience

Later today, or even tomorrow, spend a few quiet moments remembering what it was like to meditate on this station. Which emotions were dominant? What aspect of the experience stands out for you now?

Imagine
"Death"

Ravens fly overhead. Black feathers like smoke. Like a ghost in a tree, something quiet is watching you.

The one from the desert has his hands around your throat. He squeezes. You have the desert in your mouth. You thirst. You raise your head to the sky and see rivers of suffering eyes, a multiplication of sorrows. In this savage stillness, you feel it all. It burns like lightning. From your parched heart you call out to your Father, and the dark shadow disperses like fire thrown into the sea.

Then the thunder says, *He who was living is now dead. We who are living are now dying.*

The Fourteenth Station:
Jesus Is Placed in the Tomb

When it was evening, there came a rich man from Arimathea, named Joseph, who was also a disciple of Jesus. He went to Pilate and asked for the body of Jesus; then Pilate ordered it to be given to him. So Joseph took the body and wrapped it in a clean linen cloth and laid it in his own new tomb, which he had hewn in the rock. He then rolled a great stone to the door of the tomb and went away. Mary Magdalene and the other Mary were there, sitting opposite the tomb.
—Matthew 27:57–61

Jesus' Response: He Loves

Jesus has died. He has performed the great act of love: he has laid down his life for his friends. His body broken and lifeless, he is placed in an unmarked tomb. Everyone at the time believed the story was over. We know what happens next, but put yourself in the mind-set of Mary, his mother, or of Mary Magdalene or Joseph of Arimathea or Peter or any of the apostles. Jesus is dead; he's not coming back. His mission is over. He has failed.

Unbeknownst to his closest friends, Jesus is working miracles in secret, just as he's working miracles in our lives all the time without us knowing. All of this is to say that, even in the darkest hours, even when it seems that there is no hope, something is stirring behind the stone, something transformative.

As people created in the image of God, we too have supernatural powers to perform miracles—not from our own power but from the power of God that flows through us. Many of us don't believe in miracles, let alone believe that we can perform them, but that is because many of us don't try. How can we try? By continuing to do God's will, to follow Jesus every day through the successes and defeats we encounter. By never giving up and by praying to God to draw us closer to him. The closer we grow to God, the more we radiate his love and peace. And that is when the miraculous happens.

Encountering Jesus

Imagine you are there as they place Jesus in the tomb and seal him inside. Which emotions does this evoke? Imagine resting by a tree some days later and waking up to see the empty tomb. What does it look like? Do you believe your senses? What are you experiencing?

Have you ever rolled a stone in front of your heart? Try to identify a time when you blocked God from coming into your life. Write it down or talk to a friend about the experience.

Take These Words to Prayer

Peace I leave with you; my peace I give to you. I do not give to you as the world gives. Do not let your hearts be troubled, and do not let them be afraid.

You heard me say to you, "I am going away, and I am coming to you." If you loved me, you would rejoice that I am going to the Father, because the Father is greater than I. And now I have told you before it occurs, so that when it does occur, you may believe. I will no longer talk much with you, for the ruler of this world is coming. He has no power over me; but I do as the Father has commanded me, so that the world may know that I love the Father. Rise, let us be on our way.

—John 14:27–31

Review This Experience

Later today, or even tomorrow, spend a few quiet moments remembering what it was like to meditate on this station. Which emotions were dominant? What aspect of the experience stands out for you now?

Imagine
"Into the Tomb"

This desert sunset turns the sea to wine.

Your mother caresses you one more time, then hands you over to the one who would visit you in the dark, ask questions, listen. He carries your answers around with him, in his heart that now beats, in the shroud he holds, in the cloth he wraps you in like the one from long ago when angels heralded your arrival.

A slab of rock for a bed, a stone for a pillow; in this restless darkness you sleep.

But not for long.

The Resurrection

I thought you died alone, a long, long time ago.
—David Bowie, "The Man Who Sold the World"

After the sabbath, as the first day of the week was dawning, Mary Magdalene and the other Mary went to see the tomb. And suddenly there was a great earthquake; for an angel of the Lord, descending from heaven, came and rolled back the stone and sat on it. His appearance was like lightning, and his clothing white as snow. For fear of him the guards shook and became like dead men. But the angel said to the women, "Do not be afraid; I know that you are looking for Jesus who was crucified. He is not here; for he has been raised, as he said. Come, see the place where he lay. Then go quickly and tell his disciples, 'He has been raised from the dead, and indeed he is going ahead of you to Galilee; there you will see him.' This is my message for you." So they left the tomb quickly with fear and great joy, and ran to tell his disciples. Suddenly Jesus met them and said, "Greetings!" And they came to him, took hold of his feet, and worshipped him. Then Jesus said to them, "Do not be afraid; go and tell my brothers to go to Galilee; there they will see me." (Matthew 28:1–10)

Reflect

Christ says, "Do not be afraid." Meditate on these words and breathe them in and out as a silent prayer. What do these words mean to you? Do they bring you comfort? How can you help Christ continue the miracle of his resurrection in the lives of those around you?

Acknowledgments

What can I say about Loyola Press? They are the warmest, most kind, enthusiastic, and supportive people I've ever had the privilege to work with and know. Big thanks to Terry Locke, Paul Campbell, Tom McGrath, Joellyn Cicciarelli, Andrew Yankech, Becca Russo, Judine O'Shea, Rosemary Lane, Sophie Jacobucci, Denise Gorss, and Yvonne Micheletti. They are an incredible team of committed professionals and just darn good people. Thank you for everything.

I continue to be indebted to Joe Durepos—maverick, fellow-nerd, friend, mentor, and inspiration. Thanks for your advice, the laughs, and of course your camaraderie.

A word of special thanks goes to Vinita Wright. Her expert, gentle, and keen editorial eye helped organize and hone this manuscript in delightful ways. She has been and continues to be a friend and true collaborator.

Thanks to Jennifer Fulwiler and Jessica Mesman Griffith for their gracious words of introduction in the beginning of this book. These two writers are voices of a new generation of spiritual writer, and having them partner with me on this book has been nothing less than joy.

As always, special thanks to Maura Zagrans, Mitch Horowitz, Anthony Destefano, James Martin, Deepak Chopra, Mickey Singer, Eric Hafker, Michael Stephenson, Lindsay Olson, J.Ivy, Will Romano, Marty Regine, Julia Elliott, Carie Freimuth, Jonathan Ryan, Harvey and Diane Bishop, Holli Sharp, and Steve Cobb for their generosity, friendship, and inspiration.

I also want to thank my mom, Roseanne Jansen, and my sisters Mary, Annie, Julie, and Suzie as well as Fran, JoJo, Lenny, Carie, Teresa, Rob, Tina, Vicky, Joey, and Lucy, for all their love over the years. And dad, wherever you are, thank you.

Finally, I want to thank my wife, Grace, and my sons, Eddie and Charlie for their love and generosity of spirit. I've been crying quite a bit lately about how quickly time passes, but that's just because I'm so happy to spend my time and my life with you three. I love you.

About the Author

Gary Jansen is Director of Image Books and Senior Editor of Religion and Spirituality at the Crown Publishing Group at Penguin Random House. He is the author of *The 15-Minute Prayer Solution*, *The Rosary: A Journey to the Beloved*, and the bestselling memoir, *Holy Ghosts*. A popular lecturer and commentator, Jansen has appeared on A&E, the Sundance Channel, the Travel Channel, Coast to Coast AM, CNN.com and NPR. His writing has been featured in the *Huffington Post*, *Religion Dispatches*, and *USA Today*. Jansen lives in New York with his wife and two sons.

Also by **Gary Jansen**

The 15-Minute Prayer Solution
How One Percent of Your Day Can Transform Your Life

$12.95 | PB | 4407-0

The 15-Minute Prayer Solution offers numerous and wide-ranging prayer exercises that can be completed in less than fifteen minutes. And, as Jansen himself discovered, if you're willing to take just fifteen minutes a day to pray, you may soon find that the entirety of your life has become a prayer, a relentless desire to place God at the center of everything.

To Order:

Call **800.621.1008,** visit **loyolapress.com/store,** or visit your local bookseller.